What people are saying about …

DELIRIOUS

"Martin is a visionary, a leader, a dreamer, a [...] a risk taker; a man full of compassion, humility, and integrity. In this fantastic and honest book, full of wisdom and insight, you will be inspired and encouraged to live your life to the full."

Tim Hughes, worship leader and recording artist

"I have known Martin for years. I've watched his journey, shared his vision, and sung his songs. Now, in this book, we can all get inspired by his thoughts, his insights, and his hopes for the future."

Michael W. Smith, singer and songwriter

"I would recommend this book to anyone with a heart for worship. We had the great pleasure of having Martin and Delirious? lead worship at our conferences, and they truly have a heart for God. What a great story of the grace of God and what He can do with a life that is devoted to Him."

Joyce Meyer, best-selling author and Bible teacher

"Honest and humble, Martin Smith gives us a personal look at the heart and soul behind a band with limitless dreams. With refreshing honesty and rawness, he addresses the incredible tension of engaging a broken world, keeping strong roots in the church, and leading a family. It is vulnerable, prophetic, and drenched with kingdom purpose. Always pointing to Jesus, Martin Smith has had a profound influence on my life. This book has only confirmed the strong calling placed on this incredible songwriter, leader, mentor, and historymaker."

Jon Egan, worship leader and songwriter for
Desperation Band and New Life Church

DELIRIOUS

DELIRIOUS

MY JOURNEY *with* THE BAND, *a* **GROWING FAMILY** *and an* **ARMY OF HISTORYMAKERS**

MARTIN SMITH
AND **CRAIG BORLASE**

David C Cook®

transforming lives together

DELIRIOUS
Published by David C Cook
4050 Lee Vance View
Colorado Springs, CO 80918 U.S.A.

David C Cook Distribution Canada
55 Woodslee Avenue, Paris, Ontario, Canada N3L 3E5

David C Cook U.K., Kingsway Communications
Eastbourne, East Sussex BN23 6NT, England

David C Cook and the graphic circle C logo
are registered trademarks of Cook Communications Ministries.

Some names have been changed for privacy purposes.

Scripture quotations are taken from the New Living Translation of the
Holy Bible. New Living Translation copyright © 1996, 2004 by Tyndale
Charitable Trust. Used by permission of Tyndale House Publishers.

LCCN 2010940912
ISBN 978-1-4347-0237-1
eISBN 978-0-7814-0611-6

The Team: Alex Field, Amy Kiechlin, Sarah Schultz, Caitlyn York, Karen Athen
Cover Design: Scott Lee Design, Scott Lee
Cover Image: A photoshoot by Marc Gilgen

Printed in the United States of America
First Edition 2011

1 2 3 4 5 6 7 8 9 10

112910

TO ANNA,
THE LIGHT AND LOVE OF MY LIFE.

CONTENTS

FOREWORD

BY MATT REDMAN

It was the summer of 1995, and I was sitting by the hospital bed of my good friend Martin Smith. A few days earlier he'd suffered in a horrible car crash, and, in addition to other complications, his right leg was badly broken. The process by which a broken bone heals never ceases to fascinate me. Somehow during the rest and recuperation period, our amazing God-designed bodies can start to knit themselves back together, with bone and tissue re-forming and many other wonders going on beneath the surface of the skin. But what I didn't know was that in those moments of stillness, something even more powerful and wonderful was forming inside Martin. God birthed a new vision in his heart—a dream to take what was already happening through the Cutting Edge worship-music journey and commit to it more fully than ever. It was the beginning of Delirious?. Before long, the band and their families took a risk of faith, jumped out of their comfort zone, and found themselves free-falling whole-heartedly into the adventure of worshipping God through music.

The music of the D:boys started flying to the far corners of the earth, with the band touching down in as many as twenty-five different countries in a single year. The multiplication factor of the

kingdom of God soon kicked in, and they began to reproduce themselves. Every time they took to the stage or put out a new record, they
inspired many other musical worshippers to turn up the spiritual
amplifier—and find new ways of being creative for the name of Jesus.
I count myself privileged to have been one of that crowd. Watching
Martin's life and listening to his songs sharpened my resolve to live
for Christ and dream up new ways of adoring and announcing God
through music.

I knew Martin before the songs went global and the spotlight
fell on him. He's the same guy today he was back then—a thoughtful
friend and an inspiring worshipper of Jesus. I remember dreaming
together about how all this new worship music could change the
world, and him speaking many brotherly words of encouragement
over my life. He does the same today. Jesus' model of ministry
involved some huge crowds but also meant discipling the Twelve and
looking out for the individual. I've witnessed that same pattern in
Martin's life. He's brilliant on a stage, but he'll also speak God's truth
into your life over a killer homemade cappuccino.

Martin is a devoted husband to the fantastic Anna, and together
they have danced upon injustice and dreamed some big dreams.
He'll tell you so in this book, but spend a few hours around Anna
yourself and you'll realise there's no way he'd ever have pulled this
whole thing off without her at his side. There are six lovely Smith
kids, who ensure that their home is never a dull place. There's
always someone doing a cartwheel, dressing up as a superhero, or
banging away on a drum kit. *Boring* is not a word you could ever
use in connection with their home. And yet what blows me away is
there's always room for more people—I've seen many, many guests

over the years invited through their doors and shown the most amazing gift of hospitality.

Beth and I have spent many precious moments in the company of Martin and Anna, and it's always more of the same—Jesus is consistently the main topic of conversation, and we never fail to walk away inspired to run well in His kingdom. Martin has been entrusted with standing before millions, and his songs have inspired multitudes. But at the end of the day, don't let those dazzling white stage suits fool you. He's still the musical space cadet who'll offer you a cup of tea, get it started, and then wander off into dreamland while the bag overbrews and you grow increasingly thirsty! In other words, he's just an ordinary guy—who walks in obedience *on an extraordinary journey* with an amazing God.

Over the years, Martin has been a mentor to many, near and far. And in this book he will likely do the same for you. The message here is loud and clear—just like the music always has been. Martin points us to Jesus and reminds us that when we find ourselves jumping into *His story,* it's just possible we might make some *history* together.

—*Matt Redman*

INTRODUCTION

BY CRAIG BORLASE

What's the point of this book?

That's the question I asked Martin yesterday as we spent time putting the finishing touches on this book. The same question I'd asked him at the start as well, when we met in a converted crypt at the bottom of a cavernous London church. That place was so big, with so much history and influence, that it only increased my sense that this book must resound with a greater purpose.

On both occasions, Martin's answer to the question came in three parts. First, he wanted to tell a story of God's grace:

"We are no spiritual superheroes," he said, "but God took five ordinary guys and used us. All we had to do was believe that it was possible."

And then there were thoughts about you:

"We can never get far from talking about the historymakers. I want this book to help people see what's in their hands a little more clearly, to realise more fully how God made them for a reason, and that God made them with a destiny. In the same way that God took us from an unknown town on the backside of nowhere, He can take anyone and give them a life of faith and hope."

And then, last of all, there were thoughts about the broader music scene:

"And there's a bigger picture as well. We are in an amazing season where the mainstream and Christian music scenes are getting closer together. The time is coming when there will be more God-songs on the radio. We need to stop looking over the fence at the 'promised' land. So much of what we have been calling out for is here already."

When he starts talking like this, Martin can get on a bit of a roll. He might start off talking about music, but it's only a matter of a few breaths before he's on to even bigger things:

"When the world economies crash, there will need to be songs that point people to God. I spent a lot of my twenties thinking that if I just made 'Christian music' I would be somehow settling for second best. But now I see that the world desperately needs the sounds that can pry open the hardest of hearts, allowing people to know that God is God.

"It is our job to write the next songs that, like 'Amazing Grace,' will be part of mainstream and Christian culture, that shine light in the midst of the rubble in years to come."

When he talks like this, it's hard not to become caught up in it. *Yes*, I think, *I want to write those songs too.* But then I remember that I have absolutely no songwriting talent and I'm sitting with a man for whom great melodies fall from his lips like a breath.

So I ask him: What about the people who can't write songs? What about them—is this book irrelevant?

"I think that all of us have a responsibility to sing the songs as though this is our last day on earth. And we have a responsibility to live them out. Because when we sing and live together like this, uniting as one voice, it can literally shake nations. We've seen that—like the time we were in Cambodia and the government shut us down, refusing to allow us to play. But the crowd would not do as they were told. They did not walk quietly home. Instead they bunched up on the steps outside and started spontaneously singing songs to God. You cannot imagine the power that surges when the oppressed choose to tilt back their heads, open their lungs, and sing out to God. It's always been like this, from cotton fields to protest matches, from sports stadiums to funeral pyres: A cry comes from deep within the soul that wants to connect with God. *And that cry can change everything.*"

I've had the privilege of seeing the impact of the songs that have come from Delirious? over the years. I've lost count of the number of times I saw Martin take the stage, and somewhere along the line I stopped watching the band. I was always much more interested to see what was going on in the crowd. It was there that you could see things make sense, where you could see faith rise and hope receive a steroid boost, amid all the sweat and noise of the show.

It was always clear that Martin, like the rest of the band, was there to serve a greater purpose. Sure, they looked good up there, and lots of people quite liked the idea of becoming a little like them, but that was never really the point. When Martin sang about being a *historymaker,* he was just one voice in a very, very loud choir.

This book is not the definitive retelling of the Delirious? story. It is Martin's version of that band's story, told the way he remembers it. I've put my slant on it as well, asking Martin certain questions and gravitating towards particular themes. Ask the other members of the band what it was like, and their stories will be equally unique.

Read on, and you'll hear Martin's voice talking increasingly about how, lately, he has changed. He's rediscovering space, silence, and what it's like to stand still for a while. Everyone notices the change, *especially his wife, Anna.*

"Don't you think he's changing, Craig?" she asked me one day while we were standing around the kitchen, Martin doing some essential maintenance on the coffee machine.

I agreed.

"And don't you think he's much nicer now?"

I agreed with her again.

"I prefer him this way. He's much more pleasant to have around."

———

So what's the point of this book? Yes, part of it is to tell the story of the band that helped inspire a generation of worshippers, and part of it is to colour in the gaps and to show why that change in Martin was necessary, how it happened, and what it all means. But the bigger purpose, the one that reaches above us like an ancient cathedral ceiling, is to bring about a change in us all.

It's not about whether you are a paid worship leader, a kid playing guitar in your bedroom, or the lead singer of Delirious?. It doesn't even matter whether you're a songwriter: This book is about how we worship, how we live out the songs we sing.

This book is about the heart.

Everything else is secondary.

—*Craig Borlase*

1

PARADOX

I never really knew what people meant when they said that their hearts had been broken. It had always seemed to me that people were exaggerating, that the description was all a bit too over the top. But on January 10, 2007, I found out exactly what it feels like to have your heart so comprehensively messed with that you know beyond all doubt, the rest of your life will be different as a result.

For me, though, it wasn't that my heart broke. It was still beating—and faster than ever. It felt more like my heart had been ripped out. My head, on the other hand—now that was well and truly broken. Thoughts flew out like water from a broken pipe, and nothing made sense anymore.

I was a mess.

I sat in a hotel, waiting in the room for someone to take us to dinner. Nothing new there. But nothing could ever be the same. After what I'd seen that afternoon, I knew that if my world as Martin Smith carried on without any change, I'd be making the biggest mistake of my life.

We'd been in India for a day or so. In Hyderabad the band and I played to a crowd made up of four hundred thousand people, quite a few cows, and a whole lot of duct tape holding the PA system together.

Delirious? had toured India before, and we'd seen poverty around the world: We'd visited slums in Mexico and seen it from car windows on numerous drives to and from airports, but in India we always felt the greatest impact. Knowing that even our suitcases—not including the stuff inside them—cost more than a year's wages for some of these people was enough to wipe the smiles off our faces.

Mumbai was different. The sounds, smells, and general chaos overwhelmed the senses, and somehow the children's begging felt more intense and disturbing there than anywhere else. Every time we stopped at a red light and children approached the airtight windows of our cars, I wanted to empty my wallet and hand the contents over to them. It would have made the kids' pimps happy, I suppose, and I knew it was a bad idea.

So perhaps I should have known that I'd find it emotionally charged when we visited Prem Kiran, a project supported by Joyce Meyer Ministries that provides the children of prostitutes with food, education, and support. I should have known that their smiles and effervescent singing would lift my smile higher than the clouds, and I should have guessed that when we fed the children their lunch I would be fighting back tears.

But nothing could have prepared me for Farin.

You pronounce her name fa-REEN. For some reason she couldn't stop looking at me all the time that she and the rest of the children sang.

I suppose I'm a little bit used to the "strangeness" of people looking at me, but this was different. At the same time that she was looking, God's Spirit prodded me deep inside, taking my guts and wringing them out.

Once they finished singing and eating lunch, we spoke with the pastor. He told us that this project worked with more than seventy children, helping their mothers and families as well. He shared that Farin's mum—like so many of the others there—worked as a prostitute.

I felt the air leak from my lungs.

Pastor Umale went on talking. This was a red-light district, and the chances were good that, yes, Farin would end up working as a prostitute just like her mother. Seeing as she was eleven years old then, that day might not be far off.

I looked back at Farin. She was so much like my eldest daughter, Elle: same age, same height, same way of moving, same big eyes, and a similar smile. But Elle's future is one of possibilities and peace. Farin's is a parent's worst nightmare that never ends.

Pastor Umale invited us to walk across the street and visit the homes of some of the children and their mothers. We trod over the open sewer that ran between the brick and tin buildings; we wandered inside when invited and stood around looking like fools. There we were, a rock band that shouted about our faith in Jesus, standing in one room where the whole of life was played out: sleeping, feeding, playing, and working.

What did our faith mean in that place? We could take to the stage in front of hundreds of thousands, but what did our faith mean as we stood next to a bed on which a prostitute sold herself for a few rupees, and beneath which her children hid, in fear and silence, sometimes even drugged so that they would sleep? What did our faith mean, and what impact could it make? Were we out of our depth, or was that just the sort of place—and were those just the sort of people—that Jesus would have been found amongst, dealing in compassion, transformation, and restoration?

Our trip ended, and we got back on the bus. But it wasn't enough to drive off and forget about it. It wasn't enough for life to go on as before.

Back in the hotel all I know for sure is this: *I am dying inside.* Something has happened and I cannot find peace. All I can think of is Farin and the horrors that lie ahead unless some minor miracle takes place.

What would I do if she were mine?

The question makes me stop. What do I mean *if she were mine?* I realise the truth in that moment: There is no *if* in this scenario—I feel like I am Farin's father and I am as responsible for her future as I am for my own daughter's.

———

That day we spent as a band in Mumbai changed things for me, though perhaps not in the way that I first thought it would. As I grabbed a few snatched phone conversations with my wife over the coming days, all I could tell her was that something amazing, disturbing, and beautiful had happened. I tried to tell her about Farin, but the words came out all wrong.

It wasn't until the band and I got home that I had any sort of plan in place and the time and words to convey it to Anna.

"We need to adopt her," I said. "We need to bring her back here to live with us, to be a part of our family."

Anna was very good with me. She knows me well enough to let me talk and get the ideas out before those become actual plans, but she also knew that something different was going on. This wasn't just another case of Martin getting excited by someone he met at the end of a long tour.

But as I thought about it more and more, I grew even more convinced. We needed to adopt this girl. And the more I thought about it, the more I missed her. It was as if my heart—so blatantly ripped out from my chest upon seeing Farin for the first time—had now been put back but was wired up all wrong. I was constantly aware of the fact that she was still back there, living in a slum, surrounded by poverty and danger. This little girl was at risk, and I was doing nothing about it, other than looking at the photo of her that I'd placed on my piano while failing to put these feelings into song.

Eventually Anna laid it all out for me. My kids—the five we had then, sharing the house I'd been floating around in ever since I'd returned from India—needed me, but I wasn't there. Physically

I might have been in the room, but that was about it. I was drifting away, and it was starting to become a problem.

I wondered if I was having a breakdown. I struggled to concentrate and found it hard to connect with my loved ones, and all I could think about was this girl I'd only ever met once. *What was going on?*

Within a couple of weeks the air began to clear. The songs started to come—one about Farin herself and the other about her mother and her friends—and the adoption forms that I had ordered remained unopened on our kitchen table. Bit by bit I was starting to return to my body, to reconnect with the family, to come back to "normal," whatever that meant. Being in a band means that life is a strange dance. You travel a lot and develop a life made up of stages, studios, and interviews that is far removed from the realities of family life. You have to work hard to smooth the transition between these two parts of life.

But coming back from India the landing was even bumpier.

Part of me liked that idea of everything getting back to how it had been. Part of me thought it was the most frightening thing that could ever happen.

Six weeks after meeting Farin, I found out that Farin's mother had changed her mind. At the start she had been happy for Farin to leave India, for us to adopt her and bring her to England with us. Then she changed her mind. She couldn't let Farin go.

How could I blame her? Honestly, I felt partly relieved, partly upset and sad. But then, finally, something like progress presented itself to Anna and me: *If we can't adopt Farin, then let's take care of her and the other children in her neighbourhood.* The pastor told me what the project in India cost to run, and we decided to contribute: We wanted to help with the care and education of all seventy children. After all, if we couldn't bring Farin home, we could certainly help care for her along with all of her friends.

———

That is not the end of the story.

And it certainly isn't the beginning either.

The day I met Farin was one of those points in life when so many threads come together. It was a junction box, with so many different experiences and influences colliding, and so many outcomes blossoming as a result. And part of the reason I wanted to write this book was to share a little of that bigger story.

But before we jump in, I need to do some confessing. Starting with a story like meeting Farin can sound impressive. That line about having my heart ripped out and my head broken makes it sound like I'm halfway towards being a saint. Don't get me wrong—the feelings were absolutely genuine, but those were rare. On so many of the other trips our band made to projects that worked amongst the poorest people, life often went back to normal after a while.

I know lots of people who have experienced the same thing. Maybe you have too. After seeing the firsthand reality of what life is really like for so many of our neighbours here on the planet, you feel stirred up. You try your best, you try to respond to the compassion stirring within you. Most artists and creative people are by nature sensitive to suffering, and we often want to jump in and help, without thinking about whether there's a lifeline. And even if you're not a creative type, having faith in Christ more than sets us in line with compassion as a way of life.

Well, that's the theory. Or, at least, that's the start. What comes after the outpouring of emotion or the awkward feeling when you look in your wallet, that's where I think we make the hard choices.

For those of us living in the West, when we come face-to-face with poverty it can be a problem. Especially when a trip feels more like a holiday romance than a blinding light on the road to Damascus.

For example, we fly into India, stay in a nice hotel, go visit these projects, go back to the hotel, have a shower, and eat a nice meal in a restaurant, and then, if we're lucky, we get an upgrade on the flight home. In our culture, where selfishness is at worst a character quirk and at best a sign of inner strength, there is a real disconnect between head and heart, between passion and lifestyle. So we can be engaged in an issue, we can use our voices as our currency, and we can give cash. But the greatest tragedy is that we can come home from the short-term mission trip and get straight back into our everyday life *and forget*.

Not that there's anything wrong with everyday life. For me that might range from driving one of the kids to a dance lesson today and piano lessons tomorrow, to taking out the rubbish bins; from getting the car fixed, to thinking about where we want to go on holiday next summer. Everyday life for me might be planning what I'm going to be doing this time next year or thinking about how to release these songs within me for others to hear. You can forget the pain, and you can forget the faces. That breathless feeling you get when you're surrounded by life-and-death poverty can evaporate like the vapour trail left by the jet as you fly home.

I found this all to be true after my early trips to India. I didn't like the way I, like the Israelites, could so quickly forget about what God had done just days before. It might not have been a miracle like the parting of the Red Sea, but facing children whose lives were on course for abuse, neglect, and horror stirred my compassion in powerful—but sadly, kind of temporary—ways.

Eventually I found what I thought was a perfect remedy for my wandering heart. Taking photos, and lots of them. All around my house now are pictures of many of the children—God's children—through whom I have glimpsed more of life than I had known. As I sit at the piano or eat breakfast, all I have to do is look up to be reminded of their faces and to reconnect with their stories.

The truth is, though, that while the photos are a neat little device that I came up with, God had a better plan for helping me hold on to the sense of purpose that rose up after those days of seeing poverty up close. And that plan was Farin.

In one of those wonderful, God-only ways that showed how well my Father in heaven knows me, God broke into my heart and left it in pieces. Through Farin God made it all personal. And once that happened, there was no way I could ignore His call.

I'm not trying to sound like a saint again, but it's true that one day in Mumbai back in January 2007 made the rest of my life different. Of course I still have one foot in my everyday life—the world in which I find myself getting more excited about the World Cup than about rescuing kids from sex trafficking. There are many, many times when I feel as though I just don't know how to do this thing called compassion when there's so much geography in the way. All those old temptations to go back to normal. But Anna and I have come so far down a new track that I'm not so sure I remember what "normal" looks like. I don't think we can ever really go back to life being our own again.

So here we are, at the start of this book. Read it, and you'll see that I've made plenty of mistakes. I've tried to be honest with you throughout—honest about the good as well as the bad.

But, thanks to the grace of God, this book is about more than just my failings. It's about an amazing journey that I've been on. I've seen miracles, heard armies of Christians cry out in faith, and seen what happens when ordinary men and women decide to live their faith out loud.

And I hope that this book helps you unleash more of the same.

2

NOISE

My mum and dad still talk about the day. At two months old I developed bronchitis, which gradually worsened. At six months old, when my parents rushed me back to the hospital, I was diagnosed with bronchial pneumonia. I couldn't breathe, I wasn't crying—I wasn't even making a sound. So the medics took me and placed me inside an iron lung—a covered and sealed cot designed to get little bodies like mine breathing again. My parents had no idea whether I would make it out alive.

They watched me laying silent, my life in the hands of this strange-looking piece of equipment. All they could do was pray.

Their prayer was simple: "Thank You for giving Martin to us. We are willing to give him back to You, but could You please breathe into his lungs and let him make a noise?"

I guess God heard them. I guess He took them up on their offer. It was a brave prayer for them to pray, but even today they know that God has kept them at their word.

I'm one of four children, the third of three sons with a sister who is six years younger than I am. That age gap meant that she was almost raised as an only child. While the boys were off playing football down at the sports field, my little sister was at home with Mum. It was a pretty traditional household: Mum and Dad were rock solid; sports provided us with exercise and teamwork, challenges and triumphs, and the opportunity to join Dad in his obsession with the crazy English game of cricket.

And then there was church. It was always a major part of our lives, and from as early as I can remember, the Smith family would leave the house on a Sunday morning, each of us three boys dressed identically in smart shirts and ties, and complete the short walk to the small Brethren church on Canfield Road in the northeast London suburb of Woodford Bridge.

As we'd approach those big oak doors, others would converge— the men in suits, the women in hats, and the boys all in similarly smart shirts and ties. We were a little army of believers, a strong family made up of strong families, marching our way to church. Dad was always involved in some sort of leadership role, and even though there was an air of formality about the events, I never grew up with anything other than massive respect and affection for it all.

In fact, I've never really had a rebellious streak. I've never wanted to kick back against this stuff that I grew up with, and I think I've always been able to see it for what it was: *my extended family that was made up of great people who loved God*. I saw only great hearts when

I looked around me, ordinary people doing the best they could. As for the suits, ties, and hats … well, it was just what they did. It was a uniform—nothing more, nothing less.

Ever since I was a little boy, my mum and dad felt that there was something unusual about me. Perhaps they made the connection to their bedside prayers as I lay silent in hospital, perhaps they didn't. Either way, they knew that I was inquisitive about spiritual things and that I wondered why I was on the planet. I meant business from a young age, and by the time I was eight I knew that God was real and alive and that I wanted to give my life to Him so that He would use me. In some ways life has never really got any more complicated than that.

My parents didn't force me to be like this—I knew deep in my own heart that I had found God, and I never doubted that He had a plan. I was still your average naughty, outspoken little kid, but somehow I knew early on that this life is temporary and that I had a job to do. One of my friends, an evangelist preacher named Reinhard Bonnke, told me that he heard God speak to him at the age of five and tell him to go to Africa to preach. Looking at my kids today I think Reinhard's right: A child's dreams and sense of destiny begin earlier than we think. You've only got to ask your kids, "What has God said to you today?" and you'll be surprised, if not blown away, at their answers. I treat my children like normal children, but I talk to them like they are spiritual giants, because I want them to walk in bigger shoes than Anna and I ever will.

My dad was an investment accountant, and so every weekday morning he commuted sixty minutes into London, getting on the tube at South Woodford and staring into space along with all the other suits. He'd come from a reasonably well-off family (his dad was a medical doctor), and he grew up with a knowledge that church was something to which he should be utterly committed his whole life.

My mum, on the other hand, was different. She came from a poorer family in London's East End—the kind of poverty that meant she didn't get her first toothbrush until she was eight. Her mum— my grandma—was a petite, strong, and deeply superstitious woman. I suppose that like many others who lived through two world wars and saw so many men leave to fight and never return, my grandma wanted to understand the forces of life and death and avoid any more pain and suffering if she could. Strangely all her superstition fell away as she got older. Mum said it had something to do with the time when I, as a little boy, told her that she needed to start going to church after my granddad died. She did start going to church and amazingly died with a faith in Jesus.

So Mum knew about and appreciated the world outside, while Dad knew about and appreciated the world of church. They were— and still are—a great couple. Yet even though my mum didn't grow up in and around church, she has always had a profound sense of God speaking to her—even though she would never use those words. Growing up we were all used to her talking about some dream or other that she remembered from the night before. She always had feelings or intuitions about people or situations, and it wasn't at all unusual for her to have dreamed about making an apple pie for someone who needed it. So the next day she'd get up and make the pie and take it to the person she'd dreamed about, usually finding them in the midst of some kind of difficulty. Mum taught me that it never really is about the apple pie, but rather acting on God's promptings. Neither Mum nor Dad ever talked about "prophecy" or "hearing God speak" or even the Holy Spirit, but the results were the same: Mum was in tune with God and always ready to act.

Some people have said that my songs are "prophetic," that I've been writing about things to come and not just the present. I suppose that a song like "Did You Feel the Mountains Tremble?" is unusual, but just like my mum and her apple pies, I was only writing about what I woke up dreaming about. I got a sense that I always need to be obedient to God and act on what I believe He is saying. There's not much more to my songs than that.

Mum and Dad both loved God, and they still do, even though they express that love in different ways. They're strong, stable people, and they provided us with a safe, steady upbringing. My dad was the kind of guy who only ever had one job—starting it when he was seventeen and retiring from it when he was fifty-five. There were no fireworks to disturb things at home, and we would talk more about church and God than we would about Jesus. Miracles might have crept in there, but it always came back to the Word and to preaching. These discussions all went deep inside me and gave me the good basis of faith for which I have always been grateful.

This stability—with its clear boundaries—was profound. And so was Mum and Dad's generosity. Our house was like Piccadilly Circus or Times Square, with friends and strangers coming over all the time. It's the same for Anna and me today: We only know how to live with the front door half open. I learned from my parents, who were always sacrificing their time for people, always "on duty," never putting their beliefs or their principles on standby.

For holidays we'd drive to Switzerland in our VW campervan, with us kids sleeping up in the top. Or we'd go to Cornwall and stay in a Christian hotel. Dad would volunteer to give the quiet time each morning, even though we might be anxious to go to the beach, but that's what Dad did. He was solid, reliable, and dependable.

The Brethren movement always planted churches right in the very heart of communities. This meant that our little church stood in the middle of a whole string of houses. About a hundred of us attended each service, walking through those oak doors, passing two meeting rooms crammed with sports equipment, and entering the plainly decorated main hall. There was an organ and a piano at the front and a small stage with a baptismal in it. There was nothing flashy about it at all, and we'd perch on plastic chairs that we stacked when Tuesday night came around, so we could wheel the table-tennis tables out from the front rooms.

I remember the sounds of the organ. I remember the piano, too. And I remember the day we stopped singing just hymns that were found in the *Hymns of Faith* book and bought fifty copies of the first *Songs of Fellowship* book. This was a big deal: Now we were going to sing choruses instead of just the classic hymns that had lasted for generations. We were going to sing about "feelings" and use words and melodies that unlocked something fresh within us.

I was nine, and I remember standing outside the church next to a couple who had just become Christians. We were all waiting to go in, and from outside we could hear the pianist playing through a few of these new choruses. I remember the man turning to his wife and saying, "Oh, Margaret, they've just finished playing our favourite song. That's a shame, we're just a bit late."

I squeezed past them, ran in, and poked the piano player in the ribs.

"Play that song again, will you?"

"No. I'm not doing it again. I've just finished it."

"Please! Please do it again!"

I was annoying and persistent in the ways that all nine-year-olds are meant to be, and eventually the pianist gave in. I looked back to the doors and watched as Margaret and her husband heard the song start up again, their faces lighting up.

I guess I knew even then that music was powerful, that it had meaning, which could make people happy.

Despite this we didn't have a culture of music at home. It was just like the Holy Spirit and gifts like prophecy; we didn't talk about them at all in my family. Church and faith in God were about family and security and steadfastness. It was as solid an upbringing as I could hope to have had.

But eventually, something amazing did happen. Our church made plans for a weeklong mission to evangelise the local community, and someone invited a group to come along and help us out. They were called Saltmine, and they came with a preacher, a bunch of actors, and a band. They had it all—drum kit, electric and bass guitars, a big sound system. My mouth dropped open as they played the little choruses that we would sing along to on Sunday mornings, but with such energy and power! I was caught up in it—*completely*. Part of it was the power of the music, part of it was the sense of God being present—all I remember being able to think with any degree of clarity was, *This is it!*

I didn't know what "it" was, but I liked it. Something inside me was alive in a new way. And somehow, I knew that I wanted more.

We moved to a new house when I was thirteen. It was a difficult time to do this, as I'd just completed my first year at secondary school, but Dad's job moved, causing us to relocate to the other side of London. We ended up in a bigger house, in a nicer area, and there we found another Brethren church in another solid community. Dad, being Dad, filled whatever gaps the church had that matched his skills, and he soon became one of the elders and the leader of the youth group. Dad unexpectedly asked me to lead the singing in the group. He borrowed a guitar and a copy of *Teach Yourself Praise Guitar*. Overnight I learned three chords, and the next week I led the other six members of the youth group in singing. There was no big fuss about it. It was just what you did: You stepped up when you were needed.

After the evangelistic outreach in our old church, our relocation to South London, and our arrival in a new church community, things changed even more. Some of my parents' friends told them about a new event for Christians called Spring Harvest. This event was a chance to spend a week hearing about God, singing, and being with other Christians. For my mum and dad it was a whole new spiritual experience—there was so much passionate worship with people raising their hands. Honestly, I think it freaked them out a bit.

I remember sneaking into the main venue at Spring Harvest one night—it was a giant circus tent pitched in the middle of the sports field. The place was alive with the same sense that I had connected with in our little church in Woodford Bridge when Saltmine played. But this was even bigger. People around me were caught up in it, swaying gently, arms raised high, eyes closed, and faces glowing. And there onstage, leading them all, was this unassuming guy with a red beard and a guitar hanging off him, thanks to a particularly great-looking rainbow strap. He was the first worship leader I remember seeing, and Graham Kendrick would go on to become a hugely significant part of my life. Back then I had no idea of what was to come. All I knew was that I was standing in the middle of something magical.

I was home.

3

TEEN SPIRIT

I knew a few things when I was twelve.

I knew that I wanted to get baptised. I knew that I loved sports. I knew that God was real and interested in my life. And, for just a few months, I knew I felt a bit annoyed about everything. My rebellion took the form of bad behaviour at youth group. I was just starting out at my new secondary school, and like most twelve-year-old boys, I was looking for my place. For this short time I tried being mouthy to the youth-group leaders and got kicked out on a few occasions. But deep down I knew that this was not the way to behave, and soon enough the two worlds stopped clashing, and I settled into who I felt Martin Smith was meant to be: not some loudmouth thug, but a sensible kid who sought to do the right thing.

From an early age I had a sense that I wasn't quite normal. This wasn't as cryptic as it sounds, for having two older brothers who set the path in life gives you a pretty clear understanding of what is and is not considered normal. We all played sports, but when it came to God I felt different. They liked church, said their prayers, and grew in their faith. I always had this idea that I was on the planet for a reason, that I had a job to do, and that in some way this job was about God. I didn't know any more than that. As I became a teenager I took a step back from the rest of my friends' activities and tried to see the larger purpose.

So I suppose this sense of God being not only real but interested in my choices helped me get through the trials of being a teenager. Friendship struggles and school anxieties all fall into perspective when you feel as though God is calling you.

However, sometimes I felt distracted by what God had in store for me. I often felt as though I didn't really fit in. I always felt—and I still do at times today—*awkward*. Even in my marriage—which is brilliant—there's a sense that things aren't quite normal. Call it being a space cadet or just getting caught up in God-time; it doesn't really matter much how you define it. God is close, and that's all I know.

Whether I've been in a tiny Brethren church or a wild charismatic conference with thousands all around, God was and is close. And when I've stopped being busy and given God space, He's been even closer.

What it means for me is that I might be in the garden playing football with the boys, when one of my little girls hops past. Something stops within me, and it's as if I'm seeing through time into eternity. I have a lot of these moments—whether I'm standing in an arena with twelve thousand people or riding my bike down by the seafront. I carry these timeless photographs around with me, and I count them precious beyond words.

Anyway, back to the story. So there I was, age thirteen, when I started to play the guitar. I found that I could work a little and then be able to play songs. Pretty soon, playing and leading the singing at the youth group felt as natural as breathing.

Then the songs started to come. These were intense songs of love, great sacrifice, and yearning. They were songs about brokenness and pain, about separation and the eternal barriers that can spring up. And they had nothing to do with God. *Nothing at all.* Just girls.

The songs just kept on coming. There were times when I couldn't stop them, the lyrics cascading in a waterfall of bad poetry:

You break my heart when I see you,
You break my heart when I hear you,
You break my heart when I meet you,
You break my heart. You broke my heart.

I'd meet these girls who broke my heart at Christian summer camps. We'd get introduced early on in the week, hang out all week long, and then fall deeply in love just in time to pack up and go home. I was then, as I am now, an all-or-nothing guy. My whole life would stop. Completely. Bad songwriting was my only refuge.

Dad must have known that music and worship were working for me—up until then my trips to the shops with Dad were to buy cricket pads, tennis rackets, shin pads, or whatever else the next season demanded, but no longer. Now it was music that I was into. That first borrowed guitar soon went back to its owner, and Dad took me to the shop and bought me my own. It was bright blue and cost ninety-nine pounds.

The guitar shop was strange. It was a whole new experience for my dad, but for a thirteen-year-old who plays the guitar it was a magical place. For me the only thing that mattered was what the thing looked like. I had no idea about sound or build—all I cared about was the fact that it was blue and that nobody else I knew had one like it.

My blue guitar stayed with me in the bedroom, and it signified the beginning of the end of my academic abilities. From that point forward my schooling went out of the window as my brain entered guitar world. I'd come home, forget about the homework I needed to do, and settle down with my guitar. Mum would hear the *plink plonk* of my early attempts to play and would rush upstairs. She'd be annoyed, have a go at me, and tell me to get on with my homework. Five minutes later she'd be back up to see how I was getting on, only to find me staring out the window, lost in some other place.

I'm sure she didn't know whether to laugh or cry.

My parents confiscated the guitar once and stored it up in the loft. I was upset. Being separated from my blue guitar was almost as bad as saying good-bye to a girl at the end of summer camp. Worse even—there was no way I could write a three-chord song as a tribute to my grief.

I wrote and performed all my songs in my bedroom. They never made it out, which I think is for the best. There, in that little room, they lived and died.

On the wall were posters of my chosen football team, West Ham United. A couple of times each season a guy from church would take me along to a West Ham home game, and we'd stand there amongst the smoking, swearing, and emotional fans. During one match the crush from the crowd was stronger than usual, and I started to panic. A policeman pulled me out from the swell and set me down on the field. Crouched on the grass I watched as my team scored a penalty in the closing minutes of the match, sending us through to the FA Cup final. I retold the story for weeks.

I was a jock. I was captain of the cricket team and captain of the hockey team, and I played for the county at cricket and loved it with all I had. But there were some spiritual decisions to be made as well, some tensions I was all too aware of even at a young age. When you get up to county level at cricket, most of the games take place on Sunday mornings, which was a problem for me. Yet Mum and Dad never made the decision for me; instead they let me face the challenge and decide for myself. I reached a point when I wanted to make church the priority.

So I went to the coach and told him that I couldn't play on Sundays. I don't remember it being a huge issue, but a strange thing happened—they moved half the games to Saturdays, and I was able to play those games.

Despite all the matches, sports never felt as though it could be a career. There was a time when I was nine when I wanted to be the West Ham goalkeeper, but as soon as I realised I was never going to be tall enough, I canned the dream. I was never really good enough, and our culture at home had never been exclusively focused on sporting success. Church was always more important, always the foundation on which all else rested.

But music was something else entirely. Playing the guitar came easily, as did writing songs—even if they were unbearably bad. When I meet people who don't write music, I can see that it's a bit unusual to be able to pick out a melody from nowhere and craft a song. Whenever my mum is asked about what I do, she always refers back to her prayer in the hospital. I think she's right, too.

However, music was never important in our house. My dad had some albums by a guy called Len Magee, who played folkie acoustic songs, more of a spiritual rather than an artistic statement. Later on, my older brother got into ABBA, and the house suddenly had a soundtrack that was better than Len's, but we were still a long way off.

I suppose that explains why I bought my first album when I was seventeen—U2's *The Joshua Tree*. A late start by most standards, but I was getting my musical inspiration from God and church songs. Even today I'm not a massive music buyer. I'm not obsessive about it. I'm just not wired that way.

Writing songs became increasingly important, and in time I graduated from obsessive songs about lost girlfriends and turned to God. The poetry wasn't much better, but the passions felt every bit as real and even more important. "My Heart Overflows with the Love of Jesus" was the title of one. In fact, it was the verse and chorus as well.

I think I was popular at school—in our boys' schools, if you were good at sports you were invariably liked. But I was awkward with my faith. I ran the Christian union, and I was open about what I believed. But I never liked the pressure I got from the

Christian teachers to perform correctly. As the "good Christian kid" I was meant to do better, to not mess around or slack off or talk back.

One French teacher, who was a Christian, pulled me back at the end of class one day. He laid into me, telling me off for messing about during his lesson. "This is not what I would have expected from someone like you, Martin."

It got to me. I inherited my dad's sense of responsibility and always want to do the right thing. So whenever I feel as though people think I have let them down, I feel awful. This was no exception, and it left me feeling crushed.

I suppose I could have rebelled against all this expectation, and I could have turned my back on the church or family or God, but I never wanted to. Despite feeling bad when I messed up, I never really considered not being a good Christian kid. It was who I was. Why would I ever want to change?

Sixteen-year-old boys and beer rarely mix together well, and one night I had my first encounter with the combination. There was a party at a local sports club, and one mouthy guy in my class downed half a can of something and threw it all up in a drunken blur on the dance floor. He was completely out of his head. I knew that I needed to walk him home and get him safely inside, even though—or perhaps because—he was the one who always ripped on me for being a Christian. I helped him home, and as I waited for his mum to come answer the door he turned and slurred the kindest words he'd ever said to me: "Martin, I love you. You're amazing, and you know that I'm sorry for all the times I've been bad to you. I love you, mate. You're a mate."

Monday morning came around, and we were all in the court-yard, waiting to go into the class registration. In strode the mouthy, now sober guy, arms aloft like a prizefighter after a knockout blow. He was loving the fact that everyone knew he was out of his head Friday night, and he lapped up the hero's welcome.

He went over to his friends, and I heard him retell the story of his exploits.

"Yeah," he said, "Martin helped me home. What a ******."

School was just like that for me, a combination of the rough and the smooth. I tried my best to take it on the chin. Of all the rough patches, failing my exams at the age of sixteen was the hardest to deal with. I even managed to get an "unclassified" grade in music, struggling then (as I do now) to read those weird little dots on the page. I did terribly, and my humiliation was made worse by the fact that I had to retake my final year. Mum and Dad said exactly what I needed to hear—that I had to face up to the consequences of not working hard enough, that I had to work hard for the year and do the right thing.

It didn't take long for me to settle in as the oldest in the class, and I met a whole new set of friends. I retook all the exams and did a little better—passing just two more classes, bringing my total up to four in all.

But that was the year when something magical happened. I went from being an academic flunk to some kind of school hero.

One of my friends, a guy called Chris, told me about a competi-tion he had heard about and was planning on entering. A national daytime TV show was asking schoolkids to write a modern-day Christmas carol and send it in. It seemed like a good idea, so I went home and put one together, sending it in on cassette, not thinking much of it. No polishing, no refining or playing it to someone to see what they thought—I just wrote it and sent it off.

A few weeks later the school got a phone call saying that my song had made it through to the final and that I'd need to take a trip to the studios and perform it live on TV.

I was excited, but the mood changed when I spoke with Chris. His carol had not been selected, and he was upset. It was everything that he wanted to do and be, and my getting into the finals made it even harder. It was my first taste of what other people's disappointment feels like. It felt unfair: I didn't mean to get further in the competition than Chris; I didn't mean to make Chris unhappy; I only wrote a song and sent it off.

I asked the BBC to let Chris come along with me and be onstage as I sang, but they wouldn't let him come. I tried my best to make it good, to get around the fact that I felt as though I had let him down. But it didn't work.

Some years before, I had taken a few months of piano lessons from a lady at church. Like so many kids I'd gotten bored, but that experience showed me how to make interesting chords, so I chose to play the carol on the piano on TV. It was all good fun, even though a Welsh girls' choir beat me, but when I got back to school the really interesting thing happened.

I was no longer the academic flunk but a representative of the school and a kid who had gotten his face in the paper. I was invited into the headmaster's study for a chat and a slap on the back. The headmaster asked me whether I would mind singing the song in front of the whole school that week.

I remember them all—the seven hundred students and the teaching staff—lined up, with the dinner ladies and office staff at the back. I chose to use my guitar for this performance. It just seemed right somehow to be standing up there with it, not sitting behind a piano.

"Now Martin Smith is going to sing for us," said the headmaster.

I picked up my little blue guitar that had been leaning against the amp and stood before the microphone, the only barrier between me and the hundreds of identical black blazers and neat haircuts before me.

"Here we are, it's Christmas time again, here we are, it's time to meet the King," I sang. When I reached the end, there was only silence.

Today I would say that it was a tangible sense of the presence of God, but back then I had no name for it. All I knew was that it was real, and that it was good, and that I felt at home and completely surrounded by it.

I stood there with my guitar, just looking out at them. I knew that my mates who had messed with me for so many years sat out there; I could see them clumped together at the back. They were the first to break the silence, the first to get to their feet and start the clapping and cheering.

The cheering was nice, but I preferred the silence. I liked the point when there was no noise but still a sense of something louder than thunder filling the room. I liked the sense that we were not just sitting in a school hall in South London but were connected with God. I liked the sense that something bigger was going on.

I didn't have the experience to give me the words to describe that feeling. But I didn't need the jargon anyway. All I knew was that I loved the fact that when I'd played, something had happened, and that something had to do with God.

4

LORD, YOU HAVE MY HEART

As sure as I was that music was for me, I received the lowest grade for my music exams that year. I could never read those dots and lines, and my music teacher resented me for suggesting that electric guitars were a valid form of music making. I was equally sure that it was time for me to leave school. Having passed just four O-levels, including pottery, it was obvious that further study was out of the picture, and since there was no great national shortage of clay pots at the time, the future looked bad. So when the summer of my final year came around, I knew that whatever came next would have little to do with school.

Easter of that year I went back to Spring Harvest—the conference that had made such an impact on my parents and me a few years before—this time working for the company that recorded the seminars. The deal was simple: Sit at the side of the stage, press record when the speaker started, fall asleep, wake up in time to turn the tape over. In a strange way I found it exciting—I got to observe what was going on, and I liked that a lot.

A career as a sound engineer sounded good to me, and when school came to a close I went looking for jobs. I heard about a college programme that placed you in a studio alongside an established engineer who would teach you the tricks of the trade. And you got paid twenty-eight pounds, fifty pence a week. What was not to love? I managed to get a place in the programme and was pleased by the fact that the studio I'd be attached to was run by some ex-BBC guy in London.

The night before I was due to start I got a cryptic phone call saying that the studio had closed down that week, the owner had disappeared, and the placement was off. A few weeks later the full story came out: The guy had been sexually abusing young engineers and had run off hoping to escape prosecution.

God's rescue was dramatic and complete. As I recovered from the shock of the phone call I came across a plan—why not get in touch with the company I'd worked for at Spring Harvest? Perhaps they would take me on and train me.

I called them, and they agreed. So on my seventeenth birthday I left home and made the hour-long journey from South London down to Eastbourne, the ultimate British retirement community on the south coast. *Sleepy* just didn't go nearly far enough to describe the place, but it turned out that it was the British equivalent of Nashville, as the country's biggest worship label and its recording studios were both based there.

Despite the fact that I spent the first week sleeping under the grand piano while my accommodations got sorted out, the job started well. Paul McCartney was in studio for my first week, and I was the tape operator for his sessions. He was recording for a programme called *McCartney on McCartney* for BBC Radio One. The format was simple: The big man spent the entire week answering questions about every single aspect of his life, and all I had to do was make the tea, keep the tapes running, and listen to every single word he said. I was nervous at first, but soon it became clear that this was an incredible privilege and a wonderful experience.

I didn't know it then, but this was first in a series of key experiences that were to lay the foundation for what came later. It was a unique opportunity to sneak a peek behind the curtain, to see what an absolute legend was really like in person. As I listened to McCartney talk honestly, humbly, and with real gratitude about his life, it was obvious that this guy was the real deal.

I didn't just learn from world-famous music stars, because within a couple of months I was being sent out of the studio, away from the sleepy haze of Eastbourne, to a wide range of Christian events up and down the UK. Within a year I'd been exposed to every type of church and listened to every type of talk, each time pressing Record, turning the tape, not so much as falling asleep in between anymore. From black gospel meetings to charismatic deliverance conferences, Vineyard worship events to Methodist teaching conferences—you name it, I went to it.

Some events I liked, some I loved, and others I came away from feeling as though it just didn't stack up. As part of the recording process I'd have to clip a radio mic onto the speaker before they began and take it off again at the end. Occasionally these times gave me a glimpse behind the mask that some of the speakers wore. A few were rude, pumped up, and arrogant, which was a huge turnoff.

This was my Bible college—not so much listening to the talks but seeing the way people behaved. I saw the way that speakers, preachers, pastors, worship leaders, and musicians operated, and I began to form my own opinions of what mattered. I saw that what I had been brought up with was only one part of the puzzle, and it showed me that the world was much bigger than I'd previously thought.

Back in Eastbourne I ended up lodging with one of the engineers, and even though the town was full of retired people, I discovered a whole new world of music and faith. ICC Studios was home to every style of music, including local opera singers and metal bands, and I found something that I could like in every kind of music, regardless of whether they were in or out of my typical musical tribe.

The church I joined in Eastbourne was full of people who raised their hands during the worship time, just like at the big conferences I attended, but in a much smaller, more intimate setting. I liked it. It felt like coming home, and over the months it felt like some of my silent questions were answered.

One person taught me even more than any other. Remember that ginger-bearded man who led worship at the very first Spring Harvest conference I attended? I got to know Graham Kendrick well during my early days at the studio. He'd turn up and spend a couple of weeks recording, while I worked as the engineer. I saw him dealing with the frustration of the vocal-take that just wouldn't seem to work; I watched how he handled himself with humility and integrity, even at the wrong end of a fourteen-hour day. He was authentic and normal, whether under stress or not. And the sight of him on his knees at 2:30 a.m., thanking God for the take he'd just recorded, was more than enough to prove that he was a man worth listening to.

The church I'd joined was the same one that my German boss, Helmut Kaufmann, attended—a small charismatic house fellowship. One day the youth leader asked me if I'd lead worship, and my response was simple: How?

"Just get up with your guitar and sing," he said. "It's as simple as that."

So I did.

There were fifteen kids in the group, all bouncing around the small hall, and yet I felt at home again. I was pretty intense in those days, so the songs I picked were slow, brooding, intense ones: "More Love, More Power," "Take Me Past the Outer Courts," and "Isn't He … ?"

The same experience that I had in the school hall occurred when I led worship. Afterwards there would be silence and a sense of something bigger taking place. But because all this was pretty normal for the church—and because we talked about the Holy Spirit and felt comfortable waiting on God to move—it was easier to relax into it and go with the flow. Every time I led worship I felt like everything fell into place.

I spent five years in Eastbourne working at the studio, and there were some surprises in store for me. Like the band I joined. We called ourselves Hope Train, and we were a straight-up pub-and-club band.

We were all Christians, but the faith part of it was low-key. We just played to give people a good time, to sing songs that made people smile and maybe think a bit. It was fun, and it was where I started to exercise the other half of myself—*the performer*. I loved the pub environment—mixing with people who didn't know God—and I believed in what we were doing. I believed that things could happen with people as a result.

After a couple of years, it naturally fell away, as we never went beyond the pubs and clubs, but that was fine. The band ran its course. Besides, there were other songs coming up from within me, songs for Sunday morning, as well as songs for the drinkers and darts players.

It all started when I was nineteen.

It was 1989 when the first of a new series of family conferences called New Wine took place. I was sent along to record the worship, which we were going to release as an album. Up onstage was Andy Park, the worship leader from a Vineyard church in Canada. He and I got to spend a bit of time together, talking about which songs might work well on the album, and yet again I was privileged to get a close look at a man who operated with as much integrity and humility offstage as he displayed on it.

As I sat with my headphones on during the worship times I was struck—even from the first session—by the power and intimacy of it all. Typically I'd be an observer at these events—as I needed to keep an eye on the levels and the tapes to do my job properly, but it also suited me to watch. At New Wine none of that mattered. This was an experience from which I could not hold myself back. This was something I wanted to be a part of as much as possible.

I think God must have shown me that. During one session I sat there with my headphones on, lost in it all. Then I felt a hand on my back and heard someone praying.

"More, Lord. More, Lord. Come, Holy Spirit."

I didn't stop, look up, or turn around. I didn't even take off the headphones. I just stayed there, my heart beating faster, my breathing getting shallower, and my whole mind and body alive to an overwhelming sense that God was closer than ever before. In that moment God was more real, more loving than I'd ever known. I'm not even sure if I knew what was going on, but it didn't matter. All that mattered was the fact that I was able to whisper "yes" in response, over and over again.

That was my baptism in the power of the Holy Spirit. Gradually I drifted back to an awareness of where I was and what I was doing. I looked behind me, but the person who had prayed wasn't there. At the end of the meeting I went back to my bunk in a converted cattle shed and slept with a warmth and peace that I had never known.

I woke up the next day speaking in tongues. Literally. Out of my mouth came words from a foreign language that I had never heard with a freedom and fluency that I simply could not have manufactured. I knew that something had happened, that God had invaded my heart with a gentle power, and that from then on, nothing would ever be the same.

I needed to sing. I don't know where I got it, but I must have borrowed a guitar from someone, and as soon as I had some free time that afternoon I hid behind my sound desk and started to put into words and melody the feelings I had bubbling inside. It started with a chord that caught the sense of tenderness and vulnerability I felt:

Lord, You have my heart
And I will search for Yours
Jesus, take my life and lead me on.

That said it exactly. But there was more:

Lord, You have my heart
And I will search for Yours
Let me be to You a sacrifice.

And just when I thought it was over, I started to think about what I would do with all these feelings. How would my life be different as a result?

And I will praise You, Lord.
And I will sing of love come down.
And as You show Your face
We'll see Your glory here.

That was it.

I didn't know what it was, really, and I certainly didn't know whether it was any good or what it would become. I played it to a few people, and I remember someone said that I needed to change the song because "you can't start a worship song with a minor chord."

But I liked it, so I kept it just as it was.

——

That summer had a profound impact on me.

On every level—personal, spiritual, musical—I felt as if I was coming alive with greater speed and strength. The time was so significant that when a couple of years later I managed to carve out a couple of weeks holiday and save up the airfare, I flew out to North America to go on what felt like some kind of pilgrimage. I stayed for a while with Andy Park and his wife in Vancouver. I saw what he was like at home with his kids, and true to form, he was every bit as full of integrity as I remembered. I then flew down to California where I visited the main Vineyard church in Anaheim. Even from the first time I walked into the main auditorium, I knew I was somewhere significant, somewhere that, weirdly, I knew I belonged.

I was there for only three days and so only made it to one service, but it was enough. Up onstage, a poodle-haired southerner led worship in a way that I had never heard before. Again, something flickered within me, illuminating, waking me up. I saw for the first time that I could lead worship in a way that was authentic to who I was. I could be myself, just like this guy up there leading worship with a Fender Telecaster, a Vox AC30 amp, great songs, and great lyrics. The worship leader was called Kevin Prosch, and even more than I liked the musicianship and weird hair, I loved the way he'd stop songs midway through to prophesy for people. I'd never seen this before, but it instantly clicked into place within me as something that was true and right.

I later met Kevin personally and found out that the week or so before he had recorded a live album right there in the church. He was calling it "Even So, Come," and he asked me if I knew a guy called Les Moir in England. Everyone involved in worship in the UK knows Les Moir and the good man that he is. I'd been an engineer on a few of the albums Les had produced. Then Kevin handed me a cassette of the album, raw and unmixed, or unmastered, and asked me to hand it to Les when I got back.

I've been on a lot of flights back across the Atlantic since then, but I don't think I've ever cried as much as I did on that journey. With Kevin's prophetic, powerful worship on a continual loop on my Sony Walkman I was overwhelmed from takeoff to landing. Once again I knew that when I got back, some things would never be the same.

5

CUTTING EDGE

Kevin Prosch changed things. Without Kevin the entire geography of mainstream worship in the West would not be as it is today. I'm sure God would have raised up others, but from Kevin we learned that God was—*and is*—speaking through the music, and that our creativity should be unleashed in response to God rather than used to define Him, so that our lifestyles have to match up to the words we sing. Kevin taught some of those lessons the hard way.

Soon after I got back Kevin started travelling over in England, giving us permission to be ourselves, try things our own way, and create the sounds and the songs that came from our hearts. He never tried to take on the role of leader or mentor and never threw his weight around. He was in love with the idea of expressing his worship in as true a way as possible. It was infectious, and there were many of us—particularly Matt Redman and me—who loved the time we spent with this crazy uncle from over the Atlantic. When you're passionate about something you do crazy things, such as driving two hours just to spend forty-five minutes asking Kevin questions that burned inside.

It makes me sad to admit it, but I think that today many of us have lost some of the power of those days. We've become too song focused, and in truth I believe that we need to be more worship focused. We've lost the ability to push aside the songs and replace them with twenty-five minutes of crying out, opening our hearts and heads with the raw worship of God who's within us. With Kevin you never knew what was going to happen at any point in a worship session, but in church today, often six songs in twenty-nine minutes, you make sure you get your two most popular ones in there so they get a decent boost up the CCLI charts.

CCLI?

Sorry, if you don't know what that is. I'll explain. CCLI is the body that administrates the copyrights of Christian songs around the world. Christian Copyright Licensing International is a relatively recent organisation—having started in 1988—and it exists to make sure that songwriters see financial benefit from their work. I don't have a problem with the fact that CCLI exists and is very well run, but it worries me. CCLI has become the equivalent of the Billboard charts, the *New York Times* best-seller list, or the UK Top 40. People watch it *religiously* (and yes, that's a deliberate pun), and it is one reason we now find ourselves in the weird position of having a thriving "worship industry" existing today.

I've done well writing Christian songs. My music has provided for me financially, beyond what I ever wished or hoped for, so perhaps it's hypocritical of me to question the system. Frankly, I have more questions than answers about it all, and I may come back to this at points later on in this book. All I know for sure is that there was a time for many of us back in the early 1990s when worship had nothing to do with money, status, or the sort of success that could be measured by a spreadsheet. It was a time when worship songs mattered only in as much as they enabled people to draw closer to God.

I miss those days.

Back in Eastbourne, having visited the States and come back with Kevin's album filling my head and heart with excitement, I started to write more songs. I'd played "Lord, You Have My Heart" a few times at church in the couple of years since I'd written it, but there hadn't been many more songs coming up since then. After being in America, though, it was different. The first song that came was "The Crucible for Silver." I started playing it in church, and then came a song called "Thank You for Saving Me." I couldn't say that they were great songs, but they connected with people in some way. That was all that mattered, really.

Other changes occurred. At the studios I met a young guy called Tim Jupp—an enthusiastic keyboard player who played for a kids' worship leader named Ishmael. Tim lived an hour and a half away down the coast in a little village called Rustington (near a seaside town called Littlehampton), and he constantly told me about the great new event that his church was doing to connect with the community around. Tim's enthusiasm was infectious, and as we'd talk over a post-session curry or in between mixing tracks, I grew more intrigued by the church he described.

So when he invited me to stay at his home one weekend, I went. His little church felt alive in a way that I had not experienced before, and I knew right off that one day I would end up living there.

I loved the fact that they had this slightly more radical way of doing things than I had been used to. They prayed with more passion, pushed boundaries a little harder, and dreamed a little bolder than I'd ever done. I wanted to be a part of it and share in their future.

And I wanted to get to know the pastor's daughter better.

In fact, the pastor had three daughters and two sons. The eldest daughter, Becca, was engaged to Tim. Next was Sarah, who was going out with some cool-looking graphic designer named Stew Smith who played drums. But it was the youngest daughter, Anna, I liked. She came to the studios one day to sing as part of the choir for Ishmael's album. I liked her straightaway, but since I was twenty and she was sixteen it was just a bit weird, and I ditched the idea.

That's not the end of the story, as you can guess. I ended up heading over to sing at Tim and Becca's wedding, and again I noticed this girl Anna and realised again that I liked her. Out of the blue one day I got a letter from her father, David. He'd heard that I was thinking of moving to Rustington and wrote that he and his wife would love it if I would stay in their home as their lodger.

The idea was appealing—and not just for the obvious reason. I'd reached a point where I was pretty exhausted at the studios. As an engineer you work week in, week out, all the hours of the day. You eat rubbish and never get any exercise, and after five years I felt run down. I knew I needed a change, and I sensed this magnetic pull from Rustington (again, not just for the obvious reason), whispering that something profoundly exciting would be experienced there.

And so I packed up and moved into the pastor's home. There were two rooms up at the top of the house, with Anna's younger brother Jon in one room and me in the other. Jon was extremely cool in a twelve-year-old sort of way.

Of course, having fallen in love with Anna *before* moving over, at first I was a little unsure of whether I should tell David about my true feelings. As it turned out, Anna was having the exact same thoughts about me in her own head, and within a day of moving in we had declared our love for each other. We tried to keep it a secret for a few days, and I remember sitting in nervous silence at breakfast one morning, in awe of David, in love with Anna, and unsure of what to say.

David broke the silence: "I just want you both to know that I am very happy with the current situation."

That was it. No more hiding. And no more living under the same roof either. I started looking for a flat to buy, and Anna and I drove around town checking out the properties. It was strange at first to realise that we were looking together for our first home, but it quickly felt right and natural.

I realised that I wanted to be with her forever.

Anna has always brought fun to my life. I was an intense— perhaps *over-intense*—worship nerd who took things very seriously. But Anna brings light and life, happiness, and vitality to everything she touches. She is a brilliant balance to my reflective side. There have been times when I would get onstage and expect everyone to be ready to dive straight into the most profound worship experience, only to be confused and little bothered when it failed to take off.

Anna would put me straight afterwards: "You could at least have said hello to them, Mart."

When we were first married I was quite self-absorbed and selfish. My world was music, and I'd often end up being unintentionally rude to people, especially if I was supposed to take part in general small talk. Maybe it was okay to act like that when I was in my early twenties, but I'm glad that Anna brought alive something different in me as I've gotten older.

She lives much more in the moment, while I take time to process things. If we're having an argument Anna will make a grand gesture, get her feelings out, and be done with it. I'll internalise all my thoughts, but Anna will always be able to help me see things clearly. She pulls me into the present, reminds me to put the phone down and stop daydreaming about saving the world when our six children are splashing about in a swimming pool. She's taught me how to relax and enjoy life.

Anna also helps me socially. I'm a bit of a hermit by nature and would happily sit and watch sunset after sunset on my own. She's introduced me to the world of fun, parties, a full house, and late nights around the fire pit, of life lived to the max. I have to run to keep up with her. She's the very reason why our house is so full of life and so full of God.

If there's one episode that says it all about Anna, it was our wedding. I was recording in Jerusalem the week before and was a bit jet-lagged on the day. Anna and her parents pulled it all together, creating a service and a reception that was as full of life and love as any I've ever been to. We had very little money, so the whole day took place in the school hall where our church met every Sunday, and the room was full of people of every age. She had these beautiful gerberas in her hair—pinks, yellows and reds—and I stood in awe. Anna had radically turned up the brightness in my life, and it would never be same again.

Those early months in Rustington were a great time of discipleship. It was more of my strange kind of education. Where before I'd been able to see behind the stage at Christian events and get an idea of what real integrity looked like, these early days in Rustington were my opportunity to put ideas into practice, try new things, and see what worked—*or didn't*. I brought what I had to the church, and it was a perfect environment for me to grow. Anna's dad—David—and the rest of the church gave me absolute freedom to grow and experiment. I'd write a new song and try it out, then rewrite it when certain bits didn't work. I'd try cramming words into a verse of "The Message of the Cross" or load up on Old Testament imagery with "The Crucible for Silver." They just let me be myself, even if that meant having to go back and revisit songs that didn't work the first, second, or third time. I will always be grateful to them for that.

Some of us started holding worship meetings in the local school drama hall. We set up with Stew on drums, Tim on keyboards, and various bass players. It was raw, it was the complete opposite of a slick worship event, and I had a hard time saying anything through the microphone that made sense. But I have a recollection that in some weird way we *felt* like a band. Of course we weren't any good at it—at least I wasn't. I had no real experience of leading worship in front of people at an event, and seventy people was a lot more than fifteen mates from my youth group. I was nervous and awkward and didn't know whether to just put my head down and squeeze out the worship as best I could, or look up and talk to people to try and draw them in. It was a tension that would take years to die down.

But there was something right about that first event. Something powerful. *Something real and alive.*

We did loads of Kevin Prosch's songs, including "Show Your Power," "Shout to the Lord," "Banner," and "Come to the Light." Those songs set the event alight. We added in a few of my songs here and there, but Kevin's always had a mass of power about them. They always seemed to set something off in people. Now I know that the songs are just tools that help us get in the right place for the presence of God to become real and tangible to us, but in those days I stuck close to them like a little kid holding on tight to the edge of a swimming pool. If a song "worked" one month, the chances were that it would be back the next time we met.

We met once a month on a Sunday night and called it Cutting Edge. Each time the format would be the same—we would worship, someone different would speak, and someone would always share the gospel. Every time we met, kids got saved, and in a small town like ours, it didn't take long for the word to get around that something was going on worth checking out.

Within a few years of the Cutting Edge events, people talked about those early days as electrifying and extraordinary. Those times were powerful, chaotic, and experimental, but my overriding memories are that every time, we met with our Maker in a new way. We were encountering the Holy Spirit, and these visitations left an eternal mark on all of us.

But what I do know is the result of those events. Some people found faith, and others ditched baggage that had been holding them back for years. Some people were healed, while others grew into a deeper, clearer relationship with God from which they could never turn back. I know it happened because I can raise my own hand to nearly all of the above.

As we loaded our gear into the undersized hall each month—setting up in the middle of the hall so it didn't feel as though the place was half empty—there was always a sense that anything was possible. Gradually we grew used to long periods of silence, lots of tears, and even physical healings. It all grew more and more intense.

There was no business plan. There was no strategy. There was no idea even of what the next month would hold.

Years later I woke up one morning and realised that since then we'd travelled around the world, taken countless plane trips, and crisscrossed continents to sing our songs. But we'd also travelled far from the simplicity of those early days. Elements of our initial vision became a distant memory. Many great things changed, and we were grateful, but I realised that we had nearly forgotten our original goals. Having fantastic staff, owning a beautiful office building, and being able to run our own independent record label enabled us to do what we felt God had called us to do and pioneer something different. And yet things felt like they were moving too fast and I could not keep up with it all. The "machine" that we had assembled to help distribute the songs had, at times, started to dictate the choices we made.

Business plans and strategies all have their place, but that place should never come before the worship of God, our Saviour and our

Friend. The sound of our songs should never drown out the silence required to listen to God. The busyness of "doing great things for God" should never take us away from His feet.

6

SINGING IN THE STREETS

The Cutting Edge events came around quickly every month. We weren't obsessed with planning or putting on a show, but those four hours each month were so potent and powerful that they left their fingerprints on the days and weeks that fell in between.

I liked it that way. I liked the fact that church felt significant, that it felt as though we were doing something that mattered. I liked the fact that amongst us—Becca, Tim, Stew, and I, and the others who were running the event—there would be conversations that threaded through the weeks. We'd talk about what happened before, what God was doing now, and what might happen next. Every month I'd be working on a new song for the event, and they'd nearly always come out of those conversations.

"Wouldn't it be great to hear people singing in the streets?"

"Did you feel the mountains tremble when everyone shouted?"

"We need some joyful songs, maybe something happy!"

It felt as though we walked through a land that was more alive than any we had ever experienced. Not only did the songs come with purpose, but the event grew, tapping into a hunger and thirst for something new. David Thatcher, my new father-in-law and pastor, was brilliant throughout. He was a hands-off kind of leader, more like a proud parent who allowed us to run with the vision that God gave us to unchain our worship and be set free. To work as part of a team led by such a man, and put some of our conversations and feelings into words, was a privilege I will always hold dear.

I don't know if we knew it back then—it's obvious now—but the first few months of the Cutting Edge events were one of the starting points of what soon became a movement. I say "one of" because all over England things like this were happening, and people were waking up to the new songs of worship within them. All over the UK, people were experiencing something fresh, exciting, and long overdue: a sense that God was calling them to come closer to Him, to experience a deeper love and take it to the streets.

But we didn't know about the rest of the country. All we knew was our little seaside town that was a bit of a joke to the rest of the country. It was a place that had seen better days, a town that had gone from being a tourist destination for one generation to a ghost town for the next.

For us, though, it was home. It was full of people who longed to see heaven open and see God's glory come down, as well as those who knew nothing of God but needed Him more than ever. It was the place God put us, and the fact that it was isolated from the rest of the world became valuable in our lives. We could be ourselves there, a million miles away from airplanes, stages, and media tours. We were part of a family, sharing in the life of the church as the years went by.

I remember Tim driving around town in the afternoon before a service, with the PA crammed in the back his battered old Ford Escort. We'd all be there, trying to get ready for it, excited at the prospect of what was to come, but completely unable to predict what might happen.

From the first chord we had massive expectations that we would meet with God that night, that somehow God's Spirit would be tangible in the darkened school drama studio. We didn't know how that worked, but we knew that we gathered for a chance to meet with God.

My songs followed Kevin Prosch's lead. I wrote them for our little community, tried them out at the events, and put them into action in the days between. I remember vividly the first time we sang "Did You Feel the Mountains Tremble?" We played it towards the beginning of the evening, and forty-five minutes later we were still going. Waves and waves of God's power and Spirit were washing over us all. It was extraordinary, and I think it was the first time that we'd found a song with a chorus that didn't just make a statement about who God was or how we felt about Him. Instead it was a weird mix of prophecy, proclamation, and some kind of spiritual warfare. When we sang "open up the doors and let the music play," we never felt the need to add the word *please* on the end.

More than any song from the events, "Mountains" put into words and music the feelings we all shared. As we sang it over and over it eventually dawned on us—it wasn't just a song that a few people in a church were singing; this was an anthem that was being taken up by a movement.

I wrote the song in my flat a day after we'd been leading worship at an event where someone called me out and said, "Young man, I want to pray for you." When he prayed, this man said that he saw me going to poorer nations, in particular to India. He went on to say that when I played in those places, the mountains would tremble. I loved what he said—apart from that bit about India, which didn't make that much sense at the time. I wrote down the words "mountains tremble" in my journal, and the next morning the song just came.

We played it in church the following Sunday morning, in a little hall with just an acoustic guitar and piano. Afterwards Tim said, "I think that's going to work." He grinned, his smile spreading over his face.

Once you get in front of people to play songs, you quickly find out whether they work or not. There are songs on records that are not meant to be sung on a Sunday morning. It's easy to tell when you've come up with something that just isn't going to work, either on an album or live.

"The Prophet Song" was one that didn't work. The moment we played it I knew the chorus wasn't right. The verses were okay, and the lyrics felt right—the idea that "most of all, I love to hear the voice of God." But the song still needs work. Maybe I should take another look at that someday.

Soon enough we had written six songs that we played regularly at the Cutting Edge events. More and more people were asking us if they could take a copy of them with them, so it was a pretty logical decision to record them. After all, we had the studio, we had the skills between us—Stew, Tim, and I—to cover drums, keyboards, acoustic guitars, and vocals, as well the artwork, studio work, and engineering—and all we needed to do was pull in a bassist and a guitarist. That was it. Two weeks after our first recording in October 1993, boxes of cassette tapes showed up at the studio. Six tracks on each tape, wrapped up in a bright yellow cover.

Cutting Edge One was complete.

We went on to record and release three more of those Cutting Edge tapes. For some people they became underground currency, bought at the back of a school hall on a Sunday evening, passed around, copied, and played to death on car stereos on long drives home. For us they were just a new expression of the sort of worship that was rising up within us.

Each of those tapes has its own tones, its own personality.

Number one is childlike and effervescent, with no map or plan, just a collection of songs that we kicked around. It was just a bunch of demos that we recorded and mixed over a five-day period. The first tape featured the songs "Lord, You Have My Heart" and "Thank You for Saving Me."

Number two came out the following May, and it was still youthful and naive, but you can hear us thinking about it, trying to make it as good as the first one. The second tape featured some good songs too: "I Could Sing of Your Love Forever," "The Happy Song," and "Lead Me." And even more exciting about this tape was the arrival of Stu G, master guitarist with two green speaker cabs and a beautiful ginger mullet cascading down to his shoulders. He made the guitar do things we never thought possible.

Next up was the third Cutting Edge tape, released after the summer of 1994. Where number two had been purple, this one was just known by most as *The Red Tape*. It was filled with songs that were prophetic, a little stronger, and with a lot more bite. "I'm Not Ashamed" was a taste of the rock band we would eventually become, but it was the first track that gave it the edge: A single hit of Stew's snare drum and "Did You Feel The Mountains Tremble?" was off. It doesn't end for nine minutes and forty-six seconds.

I think we knew that the lyrics to that song also held something specific for us as a band. We knew that singing about God opening up the doors and letting the music play was not just a statement for the Cutting Edge events. These words were a declaration of intent for us as a band, too. It was a challenge, a calling, an opportunity to listen without prejudice to what God might be saying to us and allow ourselves to be taken wherever He led. Not only that—we meant it literally when we sang about the music playing in the streets. We didn't need to use it as a metaphor: *This was for real.* We wanted to unchain our worship and let it go. Maybe we were naive—or perhaps we were courageous—but we held on to that dream of taking it out further than the Cutting Edge events, to people who would never normally come near a church event.

The thing was, nobody had done it before. I didn't know of many bands that had made the jump from house worship band to rock group—or any worship bands that played in mainstream venues. And as for those who wanted to still keep on playing music that directly worshipped God in secular venues, there weren't any that we knew of anywhere. But we did know that we were up for it, and that along with the rest of the movement, we would use those songs to reach beyond the church.

You can hear it on "I'm Not Ashamed" on tape three, but that vision is even clearer on the Cutting Edge tape that followed. The songs are rougher, the sounds more abrasive—partly the result of our feeling more confident in our abilities. Whenever we played those songs we'd get lost in them, and so much of that was due to having Stu G on guitars. He inspired us to get better. His skill on guitar created these sonic cathedrals into which we would wander, gaze up above, and feel compelled to join in.

Stu and his wife, Karen, were living in the Midlands with their two-year-old daughter, Kaitlyn, when we met them. A year into doing the Cutting Edge events we bumped into him at a worship forum organised by a mutual friend. Tim, Stew, and I liked him straight off and invited him to come down and join us at one of the Cutting Edge events. The combination of our talents was an instant success, and we knew right away that he was our man. He fitted in well, and it didn't take long to see that Stu and his family knew a season of change was coming. Before they moved down, Stu, Karen, and Kaitlyn would come to the events, with Kaitlyn sleeping at the side of the stage in Stu's guitar case.

He was always the most talented player in the band, so he set the bar and we all had to try to catch up to join him. Over time, he started to write as well, and then we started to write together.

Finding the right bassist took a bit longer, but by the time we were ready to record our final Cutting Edge tape, Anna's brother Jon was in place. He was eighteen and at art college, and over the early years he did all his growing up from teenager to adult with us.

He became a great bassist with clever ideas, and he helped us keep questioning everything we were doing.

Eventually, we started doing worship gigs away from our hometown. We got lots of invites from around the south of England. We'd work during the week, and by the time it got to Friday lunch we'd pack up the van, head off for a gig on a Friday, maybe a Saturday, too, and then drive back home for church on Sunday.

After the third tape came out, people started to become aware of what was going on. We'd have people driving a couple of hours or more to the events, and we started to get invites to go and play at their churches. We needed a name and decided on The Cutting Edge Band. It wasn't that we loved the name, but it was better than the alternative: something with the words "Martin Smith" in it. Back in those days worship bands didn't have names. They weren't really bands at all. It was the worship leader who carried the brand, and the backing musicians were just that. I wasn't confident enough myself to make it on my own—not as a leader. I didn't feel that the Martin Smith (and Band) route was my thing. I didn't want to hire musicians to play with me; I wanted to be part of a band. Just as we were part of a movement of people, I wanted the music to come from a family as well.

Compared with the way things are done today we got off to a slow start. The Cutting Edge years were formative, with five years going by before we attempted a full-length studio album. We weren't trying to be clever by releasing tapes with just six songs; we just didn't have enough songs for more. Plus we had the studio, and we had the time. Our situation was pretty unique in that respect.

Everyone has to make their own choices and respond to what God's called them. For some bands today, like the Jesus Culture movement, they grow over a decade before coming to any sort of prominence. But others seem to be in a rush to get out there with something to sell. It worries me a bit that our songs have become less of a response to what God is doing and more of an attempt to build up the reputation that surrounds a certain church, band, or event. I know we ended up doing loads of photo shoots and having stylists and all that ourselves, but we never took that stuff seriously. It was just packaging, and what counted was the heart, *the content*. Too often today it's impossible to get noticed as a worship band unless the image is right. That seems odd to me.

Back in 1995 I was still a freelance recording engineer and producer. There was enough work to keep me afloat, and the job was flexible enough to allow me to commit to the increasing demands of being in the band. I loved cramming my gear into Tim's tiny studio. It was there that we recorded albums for friends like Graham Kendrick, The Wesley Brothers, and Matt Redman. Working on Matt's first two albums formed our friendship: All those late night chats about life, faith, marriage, and worship—and everything else—brought us close together. It's hard to imagine now, but those were the days when Matt had not played in the studio much, and his mum still restrung his guitar! He has remained a faithful friend for all these years, and he has proved to be one of the greatest lyricists of our time. We were two young men with lots of passion and lots of dreams for the future.

Towards the end of August 1995 I was on a job in Lincoln, producing a live album for a conference that was taking place there. I'd rented a truck and sat in it in front of the desk while the band led the crowd in worship. The worship leader had asked me to play "Thank You for Saving Me" on the last night, so when the session started I hit record and then ran in when it was time for me to play and sing. (I'm sure it looked very strange for anyone walking in—seeing no one in the truck, and the producer is onstage leading worship!) So I ran onstage and sang the words out:

> *Thank You for saving me, what can I say?*
> *You are my everything, I will sing Your praise ...*

Just a few hours later those words would have a greater meaning than I could ever have imagined.

7

THANK YOU FOR SAVING ME

It had seemed like a good idea at the time.

After I'd checked that the tapes were all okay and packed up the truck at the conference, we planned to drive four hours south to get home. It would be late, but it would be worth it because we'd get to see Stew and Sarah's new little baby girl, Abi, first thing in the morning. After all, she was our new niece, and her arrival was a big deal.

Anna was in the front with me, and Jon was in the back. I'd driven well enough the whole way, but by the time we neared home I was fighting the desire to shut my eyes and sleep. I played all the usual tricks to keep myself awake—the singing, the gum chewing, the head shaking—and it had worked. But as we pulled onto the main road at a little after 2:30 a.m. to drop Jon off, I must have relaxed. I switched off and went blank.

The next thing I remember was waking up.

The engine was quiet, but there was sound filling my ears. Where I was I couldn't tell you at first, I only knew that something was not right. I felt with my hands to the side of me. There was the car door, its mixture of fabric and metal familiar to the touch, but something was not right. What used to be smooth was now bulging and broken. I opened my eyes to see, at first, my hands in front of me.

That's good, I thought. *My hands are there still. I can still play guitar.*

I looked down. Something was not right with my legs. I could not see them. From my waist down, there was just a heap of junk. Somebody must have put a bag on my lap. Why would they do that? Why would someone put such a thing there?

I could hear something, a little distant at first, then clearer and nearer.

"Help! We need some help here!"

That sounded like Anna.

I turned. She was not sitting next to me. I looked up, and things became a little clearer. The windshield was shattered, and I smelled fuel. This must have been a crash. A bad one, too. I looked down to see if I could do something about shifting this bag from my lap and get out to help Anna. It was no bag on my lap. It was the dashboard.

This revelation opened the door to the pain. My back was telling me that things were bad, but how bad? I remember the pain got worse, then the paramedics and fire brigade arrived. Someone gave me some morphine, and after that I don't remember much.

I woke up in hospital, and Anna explained what had happened. I had fallen asleep for only a few seconds, but it meant that I missed a bend in the road and ended up driving head-on into a brick wall. She and Jon had been able to walk free from the car with only minor injuries, but it took the emergency services an hour and a half to cut me from the truck. Later on I found out that when the teams arrived at the scene, few of them thought I'd make it out alive.

But I did. I had broken my right femur, and doctors opened it up and pinned it, but that was pretty much it. After two weeks in hospital I was out and home again. These days I have deep scars on my kneecap and a huge scar on my hip where they put a pin in. These remind me daily of what happened that night as well as the healing that took place in the days that followed.

Those two weeks were significant. People kept on telling me that I was lucky to be alive, but somehow that word *lucky* didn't fit. By all rights I should have been dead, and as I lay on the bed, listening to the squeaky floors all around, the whole event seemed way more significant than just finding an extra twenty pounds in your wallet or avoiding the construction traffic on the way home.

I knew this was not "luck"—*this was God.*

The night of the crash I'd been singing "thank You for saving me," and now it was clear that God had done it again—He had saved me from death. The question was, what was I going to do about it?

My friend Les Moir came to visit me, bringing a book to help pass the time. It was *U2: At the End of the World,* an authorised biography of the band by a journalist who had spent three years with them. The author had seen them up close and personal, watched them work behind the scenes to bring about change, and watched their passion for inspiring an army of people to do the same.

At the same time I had the words "open up the doors and let the music play" running through my head. There was a connection between these three elements: the concept that God had rescued me, the idea that there was a way of using music to connect with people on a deeper level, and the prayer that God placed within all of us in the movement that He would open up those doors.

The crash was more than just a collision between metal and brick. It was the point at which my life changed forever.

This was the first time that I'd been in hospital since being admitted as a six-month-old baby. Here I was twenty-six years later in a similar sort of place. Only this time it was my responsibility to offer my life back to God. It was up to me to pray, up to me to lay down what I had and get real with God. I could either carry on or take a risk and make a jump.

People say that a hospital bed is no place for making life-changing decisions. I don't agree. I think it can be the ideal place from which to take a look at life and dream up a plan for what could come next.

I asked Stu G, Jon, Tim, and Stew if they wanted to go full-time with the band. We had already been pooling our skills to keep things running—Stew and Jon could handle the visuals and the merchandising, Tim dealt with the business side of things, while Stu G and I knew enough about sound, songwriting, and production.

We'd been busy enough over the past few months to know that there were enough bookings out there to keep us financially afloat. We also felt that the bookings would increase once we started telling people that we were available. But it was not just about doing slightly more than we'd done before: I was fired up with this sense that if we took this risk now, something incredible might be around the corner. This was our time—our time to walk the plank and see how far all these great ideas and God-sparked fires could go. We might even end up making an album.

Actually, we were more ambitious than that. We'd already been asked if we wanted to sign to a record label, but we'd resisted. It just didn't seem to make sense to us. Sure, there was the support that you would get from a label, but from the very start when the first run of tapes sold out within a couple of weeks, we knew that this was an underground affair. The people who bought our music didn't necessarily visit the Christian bookshops that the record label would get us into, so why sign away a whole chunk of independence—and money—in return for something we didn't need?

Throughout the whole time we were a band, we never once signed to a record label. We had distribution arrangements, and we always kept control over the music we made. It meant that we kept our independence and were able to make important decisions, like how often we travelled away from home.

If I'm honest, there was also a part of us that wanted to buck the system. In addition to the noble cause of making our families a priority, we also quite liked the idea of being this young upstart band that broke the rules and showed others what might be possible. We were on a mission from God, and we didn't want to compromise one bit. We were a great team, and it's amazing to think that we did most things in-house. I'll admit, though, at times we could have benefited from outside opinions. We could have used some fresh perspective, not just spiritually but musically. I look back and see that every

album had one song that should have been left off. A record label
could have brought perspective like this, but we were our own label.
I sometimes wonder what we could have done with being kept on
track a little more, keeping our focus tight on what God called us to
do, but we did what we did, and we did it with the best of intentions.
We always wanted to do the God-thing.

By three months after the accident, we had all agreed: *We'd do
it*. We would sell our businesses, ditch our gear, and form a new
full-time band. We'd be known as … well, we didn't know. We didn't
have a name. We knew that the name The Cutting Edge Band wasn't
the right fit for us, but what else would work? We asked around, but
nobody had any great ideas. And then, somehow, we decided to call
ourselves *Delirious*. Then Stew added a question mark to the end and
a *5* instead of the *s*.

Even our name broke the rules, and we liked that.

Just a couple of months after the accident, in October 1995, we
recorded and released the final tape as The Cutting Edge Band. We
called it *Fore* because someone told us that's what you say as you fire
a golf ball down a fairway and it's at risk of hitting someone. It wasn't
that we thought our aim was bad, but we liked the idea that what we
were doing was a little "dangerous."

Listen to those six songs now, and you can hear that building
sense of optimism and momentum. "Louder Than the Radio" is up
there at the start of it all, fixed on the idea of the music breaking out
of its confines, while "Shout to the North" is a simple reflection of
where we were as a church. But the other four tracks tell a different story—the story of a second chance. "When All Around Has
Fallen" and "I've Searched for Gold" say it all in their titles, while

"Obsession" and "All I Want Is You" tapped into some of how we felt at the time: fragile, dependent, and shaken up.

All the time I was recovering from the accident we discussed what it would be like when we went full time. There were no real arguments against it. However, one person, who wasn't in the band, thought it was a bad idea.

"Nobody makes it full time in Christian music in the UK," he said. "You've got to have a sideline, something to make you some money so that you can tour on the weekends."

I understood what he meant, but he hadn't understood the future as I had glimpsed it: abandoned to God, letting the music play in the streets and feeling the mountains tremble. What room was there for safety nets in that kind of dream?

The simple truth is that we felt invincible. Not in our own strength—I still had the crutches and scars to remind me of my own fragility—but in God's. We were off to save the world. We were going to respond to the call that we had heard and join the rest of the movement to get beyond the walls of the church. A little over six months after the accident we cut the ropes and went full time, and the journey lasted another fifteen years.

8

AND THE MOUNTAINS TREMBLED

The days that followed were phenomenally exciting.

The Cutting Edge event had grown from a single monthly meeting in Littlehampton into a series of regular events along the south coast in Portsmouth and Southampton. I knew of friends who would wait in line to get in, their hearts beating with anticipation. Some would drive four hours to make it to the event; others would stand at the side, silently soaking it all up. Some danced, some didn't. There were no rules.

One night we played in Southampton Central Hall, and something amazing happened. The night before I'd dreamed about someone in a wheelchair. The dream held nothing more than that, I simply saw someone turning up at the event and being unable to walk. Honesty, the dream slipped to the back of my mind during the day. But as the event got under way, the image came back. I could still see it, still sense it the way I had in the dream, and I knew that I had to say something.

As one song ended, I spoke up.

"Um, I think that there's someone here in a wheelchair."

I wasn't looking up at this point.

"And I believe they need to walk again."

Right at the back of the venue a little hand went up. It belonged to a girl. From where I was standing she looked like she couldn't have been much older than fifteen, but it was hard to tell from the stage. Especially as everyone around—in fact, everyone in the whole venue—turned to face her. As if guided by some voice I could not hear, they gradually all lifted their hands and reached out to pray. This was the people movement in action, not needing to be directed or instructed. We were united in our belief that God's presence was stronger than ever. You could sense the faith in the room; you could almost feel it between your fingertips. I've never known anything like it.

I knew that I needed to pray. All I could think of was to say the kind of thing that you might read in the New Testament:

"In the name of Jesus, get up and walk," I said.

The next thing we knew, the girl stood up. And then she's running around. Not just jogging, but leaping, bounding, as if the gravity beneath her had been slashed in half. It was the most emotional moment that I can remember. So many people in the room were crying, and at that point, at that time, the levels of faith were so high that it felt as if absolutely anything could happen.

I never got to see what happened when her dad came to pick her up—I was packing up the gear—but my friend Billy Kennedy told me that he saw her running into the arms of her father. He walked into the lobby ready to wheel her out to the car, and there she was, running into his arms.

I think that the girl had been effectively paralyzed from the waist down and the prospect of her walking was, according to the doctors at the time, zero. As far as I know she is still walking today, and she never did have to use that wheelchair again after her father put it in the trunk of his car.

There were other stories like this to come. Tales of depression that lifted, of hospital bedsides made more hopeful, deaths made a little easier by the soundtrack of songs that grew out of the movement of people towards a stronger, clearer view of God.

Once, we asked people to write in with any stories they had about how God had touched them through the music. It wasn't a vanity exercise but a chance for us to find out more about what we had always heard whispers of. The response we got was amazing.

It was my second year in high school, and it seemed as though my whole life was falling down around me. I was contemplating suicide. But then I happened to be listening to "When All Around Has Fallen." It gave me hope. I had a talk with one of the only friends who hadn't hurt me and she, along with your song, helped me through it.

In April this year, my sixteen-year-old sister died unexpectedly. I felt grief and anger at God. Later, I was listening to *D:Tour Live* and heard "Summer of Love." The song seemed an answer to prayer—it reminded me that God was there, and He still listened and cared.

It was early afternoon, and my mom had taken my father in for a check-up on his cancer. About an hour or so after they left I remember getting a phone call from my mother telling me they had to rush my father into surgery: The cancer had spread, and they were giving him very little chance to live. They were left with no choice but to take the risk and perform surgery. She told me that he had twenty minutes before they actually put him under and took him in for the operation. So if I were to hurry I could make it there to see him before the operation. I jumped in my car, and "Find Me in the River" came on. It just broke me. It dealt with my own personal need to seek a deeper relationship with my Saviour, and it also made me face the reality of my father's need for salvation. I left that song on repeat for the rest of the ride to the hospital, and even though I ended up missing my father by a few minutes, when I got there I had a peace that everything was going to be all right. He did end up making it through surgery, and I was able to get a little over a year longer with my dad before he passed away in September of 2000. When he died he went to be with the Lord. The month following his surgery my pastor led him in the sinner's prayer, and every time I listen to "Find Me in the River," I remember my dad and those moments.

At the age of fifteen, I had "suffered" or "persevered" through M.E. (myalgic encephalomyelitis) for five years, so for me 1996 was a milestone year. I was well enough to sit at the back of the synergy meetings at Grapevine, and Delirious? were leading worship. My youth group moshed at the front. Some guys came and prayed for me. As "Find Me in the River" found me on my knees, the energy that had so been drained poured back into my body. The next day I was up there jumping to "I'm Not Ashamed." The healing process took around a year altogether, but I thank God for how He used Delirious? and how He met me that night.

I have always been drawn to the intensely personal worship put forth by Delirious? since the moment I was first introduced to your music with *King of Fools*. I was hooked; the words and music were "where I was." I would listen to it all day long at work. *Mezzamorphis, Glo, Deeper*—the attraction continued. Particularly, it was "Jesus' Blood" and

"What a Friend" that got into my bones. Simple songs that said volumes! These songs saved my life during what was the most "Job-like" experience I have ever had. Three years ago, my younger sister, who was thirty-four at the time, suffered an aneurysm and a stroke. The surgeon said that chances were she would not survive long enough to get surgery due to complications that prevented them from performing immediate surgery. During that week of waiting, life was very surreal. I survived on prayer and worship. Six days later she had surgery. Shortly after surgery she went into a coma. A couple of days after that, our family was summoned into a small room and told there was no brain activity and that she probably would not survive the afternoon. Desperate, angry, lost, and alone were just some of the feelings churning inside me. Exhausted of this battle, I drove to my church and just sat in the parking lot, listening to your music, crying. "Jesus' Blood" and "What a Friend," I played them over and over. The tornado of emotions gave way to His presence. I was not alone. She spent two months in that intensive care room. I would sit by her side and sing "What a Friend" to her every day. She survived, but had the outcome been different, I know I would still consider Jesus my friend. His blood did not fail me!

It was—*and still is*—the most humbling part of all this. To be given the ability to write a song or put together a melody is one thing, but to have God take those little songs and work through them is profoundly moving. But even more moving is seeing the people movement rise up and live their faith bolder, braver, and bigger than before.

Of all the stories, one has a particularly special place for all of us in the band. We first heard it, quite out of the blue, when her pastor sent us an email:

> My name is Matthew. I am twenty-five years old, and I am the music pastor of a small-town church. I wanted to share with you a story of how your music helped to bring physical healing and spiritual renewal to our little congregation. You see there is a very dear friend of mine here, a girl named Jessica, who about four years ago became very sick. She was fifteen years old then. The doctors did every test in the book to find out what it was but could come up with no answers. Her hair all fell out, her immune system quit functioning and actually began to attack itself, resulting in a very debilitating condition. Then it shut down altogether. For four years she spent most of her time in the hospital, weak but very valiant and very much abiding in the sufficient grace of God. We raised money to send her to the Mayo Clinic in the United States, but even there the doctors were left confused and unable to help

her. It seemed the more medical help we tried to get, the less hope there was.

Now here's where Delirious? fits in. Throughout this illness there have been several times that God used the song "Did You Feel the Mountains Tremble?" to bring confirmation to Jessica about different things in her life. It seemed that the song would always pop up at precisely the right time and remind her of God's faithfulness. So this song has become very special to Jessica and has always been a favorite of our congregation.

About a week and a half ago, I got a call from the hospital saying that Jessica had been asking for me. When I got there I wasn't prepared for what I saw. She was in the worst state that I have ever seen a person in. She was so weak that she could barely speak; she weighed about thirty-nine kilos [approximately eighty-six pounds], as she had been unable to digest food in her stomach for about eight months. She was fed through a tube and had two permanent IVs put into her abdomen for pain medication. She was also racked with seizures so painful that she was screaming for God to take her. She had almost no control over her body and was so drugged up she rarely made sense even between seizures. Also at night she had been having extremely frightening attacks where there would actually be demonic manifestations and she would lash out with hateful and blasphemous words and try to attack everyone near her bed. The doctors gave up and said that there was nothing more they could do.

After I got to the hospital her seizures lessened a little, and she managed to ask me to sing "Did You Feel the Mountains Tremble?" So there in the hospital I sang for her, and she calmed down and began to worship with me! Then she asked me to pray that God would give her a clear mind to be able to speak and understand. God answered our prayers, and she was clear all day, despite being on enough drugs to knock out an elephant! Throughout the course of the day she made me sing that song about ten times, and about the eighth time, God spoke to me, and suddenly I realised that there was a prophetic word in the song for me and for the church. The last verse, "Do you feel the darkness tremble?" God used to affirm in me some things that I have been trying to figure out about faith and healing.

I asked God why He hadn't answered our prayers for healing, and He answered me. He said, "I have answered your prayers; just take a look at what you've been asking for!" And I realised that I had been praying faithless prayers: "Dear God, please heal Jessica, but, if it's not Your will, then just bring people to Yourself through her sickness."

God answered this prayer by many people becoming Christians through Jessica's testimony, but the problem was this—basically we were saying, "If she lives, that's great, but if not, that's okay too", and I realised what a faithless prayer this is. No matter how God answers, we win. I really sensed God wanting us to pray honestly before Him—that truly all we want is for Jessica to be healed and for God to get the glory. And as the body of believers that surround Jessica, we all needed to be in agreement with our prayers.

I shared these thoughts with our congregation this Sunday morning, and they agreed with me that we had been praying double-sided prayers. As a congregation we sang "Did You Feel the Mountains Tremble?" praying that God would affirm the message of the last verse in our hearts, and then prayed as best we could for Jessica's healing. On Friday, two days before, the doctors had disconnected Jessica's food supply due to an infection and said that she had two days to live.

That was six days ago. Jessica is alive and recovering! Her immune system began working again on Sunday for the first time in four years, and the infection went away! Praise the Lord! She is daily getting stronger and has been able to take liquids into her stomach for the first time in eight months. Also her hair is growing back, which the doctor said could not happen! Praise the Lord! I went to see her today, and she is already much stronger than she was even yesterday! The doctors have also reduced her pain medication, and her body is beginning to return to normal! There is still a long way to go for complete healing, but we are still trusting and believing for this miracle to come to completion.

I live for those moments more and more, for the times when heaven breaks through and what is broken is made whole. I believe with conviction that I'm personally in that time again, a time when God breaks into our everyday lives. Not that I ever left it, but as a band sometimes we could make such great sounds together that there wasn't always enough room to allow God to take full control.

This is nothing new, and doesn't it affect all of us in some ways? We can get "good" at what we do, whether it's work, bringing up children, or marriage, and in that routine and ritual we can forget to stop and let God in.

But no more. Those days are here today. The time for letting go and letting God take over is here again.

We see fewer healings in the West than in the developing world, maybe because we can go to the doctor, the health centre, or pharmacist. People around where I live don't suffer from malnutrition, typhoid, or cholera because we've created a standard of living that insulates us from those diseases. Is that a miracle in and of itself? Is heart surgery a miracle? Or do these things allow us to keep God at arm's length? It's all too much for me to work out, but I know that we in the West feel like we have fewer divine interventions. I don't want to write off the miracle of medicine, but I do believe that it does make us feel less dependent on God. We don't stay up for days on end crying out for God to heal our broken bones; we just go to the hospital and get them fixed.

Maybe it's less the medical stuff that keeps us away from God. Maybe it's this culture we live in. We can have a nice life—a very nice life; we can get by. We don't need God. Or, at least, that's what we seem to tell ourselves.

We live in a time of celebrities and instant fame. Magazines tell us the lifestyle choices that we need to make, and Twitter allows us to break in to the inner worlds of Ashton Kutcher and Demi Moore to find out what they're thinking. But even though we might feel as though we are living the dream and making life our own, too often we're just following the script that keeps the marketing executives happy.

But we who serve the greatest Leader of all, who pledge allegiance to the Servant King Himself, don't need to blindly follow these little idols. We shouldn't need to validate our self-esteem through worldly fame, and we don't need to limit our horizons to whatever we're told to want.

The stories I've been telling in this chapter get me every time. These are all as different and as unique as the people who wrote them, but they share one thing in common: They speak of the glorious power of God—a power to break limitations and transform broken lives.

That's what I want to chase.

That's what I want to follow.

9

WHITE RIBBON DAY

I was at home at the time, just watching TV. It was easy to grow immune to the pain and suffering experienced by so many people living in Northern Ireland, and calling them "the troubles" just sounded like a bad euphemism to me. The random killings, brutal bombings, and unveiled hatred that flowed out of the sectarian divisions in the country were all far more than "troubling."

It was a tragedy, nothing less.

On the TV I saw a news story about the thing we called the Peace Process. Now this was no euphemism, as peace was indeed the only goal worth pursuing. It was a long affair—at times moving forward, often moving back, all the time showing just how much God's healing and restoration was needed to bring the country back from the edge.

A politician appeared on screen wearing a white ribbon on his lapel. It was a sign of peace, he said, a sign of the nonviolence, openness, and cooperation that was the only way forward.

Then he said something that lodged itself in my brain and refused to leave:

"Today we are praying for white ribbon day."

I loved the line and wrote it down. It made me think about the life of Jesus, about how He's the real peacemaker, how He was—and is—the answer to our conflicts and hatreds. I'd grown up, like so many others, with a view that politics was best left to the politicians, while God directed the lives of the faithful Christian believers as they gathered in church. Perhaps that division wasn't as clear cut as I'd thought. Maybe things weren't quite that simple. Could it be that the world needed to hear the language of the church? Were there others who understood what it meant to "open up the doors and let the music play"?

I'd often thought that revival meant blinding shafts of lights piercing the sky. But I've grown to see that there are others signs, such as lives being transformed. Surely one of the symptoms of revival is seeing people released in the fullness of their calling or gifting.

Amongst all that transformation I've come to see that politicians play a unique role in the kingdom of God. The policy of a government can influence the moral compass of a nation. But we can be tempted to forget about the politicians, particularly in the UK where we are often told—*wrongly*—that faith and politics don't mix. We can rightly pray and protest for the lives of unborn children, but we also have to support and pray for the lonely "propheticians" who campaign tirelessly to see moral decisions made at the highest level.

Life in church is often very black and white—and this is good—but politics can occupy a grey space that leaves these campaigners isolated and misunderstood.

———

We were just a worship band. But we had a sense that "worship band" was a title that could have influence in more than just church halls. We had a sense that the old definitions just didn't work anymore.

And so, somehow, a fresh idea took root: We could release our song "White Ribbon Day" as a single. We'd never been on the radio, in the paper, or anywhere near a TV studio or one of those proper venues where they stick your name up in lights out in the front. We seriously thought about releasing a mainstream single that included the words "hallelujah, hallelujah, hallelujah," right at the very heart of the action.

Like I said, the old definitions just didn't seem to work anymore.

So, we got ourselves some white ribbons, found out about how to get a single released, and set to it. We'd become friends with a guy named Tony Patoto—a Canadian working in London for a big record label. He was a man we knew we could trust instantly, and the day he quit his job and agreed to be our manager was a key milestone on our journey. He brought professionalism, confidence, and the biggest set of shoulders we'd ever seen.

With Tony advising, we put "White Ribbon Day" out as a single. The song hit number forty-one on the singles charts in the first week and then backed out after that, largely due to the fact that we had distribution issues. Basically, we couldn't get enough copies into the shops. I remember us all being disappointed. After all, we were only one place short of the magic Top 40, which would have guaranteed us play on chart rundown shows and our name and single title in the papers. It felt as if it wasn't quite our time yet. However, we were encouraged to keep going, and the more we talked to people the more we had a sense that the people movement was right there with us. Everyone talked about feeling connected to a new expression within the wider church. They began to see that they were part of something bigger, that we could all be both local and national.

I think that in "White Ribbon Day" you can see the beginnings of what we later became. We were desperate not just to sing Jesus songs but to take on the wrongs we saw in the world and to do what we could to make them right. People often ask me about the roots of CompassionArt—a gathering of songwriters and artists that Anna and I initiated in 2007. The roots of CompassionArt have to do with our trips to India, Cambodia, and Rwanda. These trips were important experiences, but the true start of the CompassionArt story snakes all the way back here, to five blokes singing about a century-old conflict that had claimed more than three thousand lives. We didn't fully understand this conflict, but we knew we had to sing about it. When things around you are not right, you use your voice to speak out, and you pray. So that's what we did, just like the rest of the church has done for generations.

We were crazy to think that "White Ribbon Day" would ever get in the charts, but at the time we felt invincible, like we could take on whatever system stood before us. We honestly thought it would be a number one. Who knows where it would have ended up without the distribution problems?

We'd talked about it at gigs, but we'd made a decision right from the start that we did not want to somehow guilt people into buying the single. If you liked the music, *great*, but the last thing we wanted was for people to feel as though it was their Christian duty to spend their hard-earned cash on our song. That tactic had been tried in the past in the UK, with some success. But again, we wanted to do something different. We wanted—if we were right about where we thought God was leading us—to become a band whose voice was heard within the music business. We embarked on a long journey, and we were OK with those first steps being small ones.

The other Christian band that had made it into the charts—Heartbeat—had also made it onto the most important TV programme in British pop history: *Top of the Pops*. We felt like we should be on the show also, not because we deserved it but because we were convinced that Christians shouldn't shy away from being open about what they believe. Christians need to get out and be a voice in media, entertainment, and culture just as much as in politics, the legal system, education, health, and social services. We are not meant to hide away; we are meant to be leaders.

I never thought that we wouldn't be on *Top of the Pops*. I felt an absolute total conviction that God would do it. That youthful zeal meant we didn't always stop to think through things, and we could have taken more time to pray about various decisions, to seek God's absolute will. This is just my opinion, but I look back and think that once or twice we got carried away on the wave of excitement and chose the wrong route. We knew that God had a unique plan for us, but it's hard to keep your head when Virgin Records calls you. I think we took a few wrong turns and made a few detours for ourselves. But hindsight's a wonderful thing.

We were determined not to sell into the church as though it was a mission project. We wanted to stand or fall on our merits and God's grace, not on our ability to persuade Christians that God was on our side.

In these days we held on to the knowledge that God called us to what we were doing. We put the band ahead of other careers, our reputations, and even—to a certain extent—ahead of our families. Some of these choices felt like sacrifices, some less so. Some were sacrifices we made ourselves, while others had to be shouldered by our wives and our children. Our seventeen years as a band asked a lot of those we left at home for long periods of time.

As we started to get out and talk to journalists and other bands (particularly those in the United States) we began to realise that we were different from other bands, and not because of our faith—we met plenty of people who had that. We were different because of the strength of our connections to our home church. If we were to chop off the roots and head away to become a rock-and-roll band, I knew we would fail.

A mainstream journalist asked me once: "Why do you still have a love for your church roots? You're good enough, so why not just forget it all and become a great rock band?"

I pondered his question.

"I think we can do both," I said.

He didn't quite know how to respond.

Maybe he was right. Or maybe he was wrong and we were right. I do know that all of us in the band are still married, and we value more in life than adulation and fame. It's been really important to us for our children to grow up in a strong local church. Our world is not totally consumed by music, and not even by "saving the world" with our music.

It didn't take long to discover that in America the typical way Christian bands worked was to spend the bulk of their year on a tour bus, sometimes playing 250 dates a year. We'd only ever do a maximum of ninety gigs a year, and we'd fly everywhere, all the time giving into the gravity of getting back home. Our rule was that we would never be away for more than ten days at a time, and once a month we'd always be on the rotation to lead worship at home.

There is an irony about writing worship songs: You write them for your local church and find that they make connections with people from other churches. The stronger those connections, the more time you spend away from your home church—the very place where those songs were conceived, born, and nurtured. This can lead to a feeling of disconnect, as if two parallel worlds are fighting for the same space.

At our home church we never wanted to be anything other than regular members of the community. We didn't want special attention, and for some people in the church there was far too much attention given to us, while for others Delirious? wasn't spoken about enough. I can sympathise with both views.

All of us in the band experienced the heartbreak of leaving children crying on the doorstep as we climbed into the bus and headed to the airport. Sometimes the darkest, most depressing times of all were on the journey to Heathrow Airport, as all of us sat in silence, fighting back tears.

Were we right to go? Were we bad fathers? Was it okay that our children and our wives had to deal with the struggles that came along as a result?

Was it right that even though we blessed thousands of people whenever we went off on a trip, our children had to go through the pain of separation? Was this the mark of a good husband—one who followed his heart—or a bad one, the sort who allowed his heart to harden just enough to get onto the bus?

I would say that for all five families involved, it was a good experience overall. At times we travelled together: seventeen children and ten parents living in three tour buses as we toured the States once a year. Experiences foreign to most children became regular occasions for ours. Also, I am humbled and excited by the fact that my children have seen God move powerfully in many different cultures with many wonderful people. Even though there were painful and difficult times, if you talk to any of my six children now, they have a positive memory of their dad being the singer in Delirious?. I put this purely down to the grace of God.

If you're a band in England, then things automatically become international. The same is not true if you're a band in the States. You can work hard all year round and never once use your passport.

And these different cultures have a significant influence on the bands they create. For the bands in America, notching up 250 tour dates a year, they understand that they frequently take to the road for three months at a time. It's a great way to get out in front of lots of people, but a rubbish way of keeping yourself rooted in a community of fellow Christians. I've met many bands who tour this way and who simply do not make it to church services at all during three-month-long tours. They might go into lots of church buildings, but that's no substitute for going back to your spiritual home, having people check how you're doing, and worshipping with friends in front of whom you have no pretensions. There's nothing like being a part of a community, and in my opinion, extended periods away from home only seem to leave people weaker. It allows people to develop a parallel universe that exists only on the road, and it's easy to be unaccountable to others in that place. You can sense it in some bands, and you see the signs in their lives when you meet them. You can hear it in the music, too; three albums in, and it can become a hollow, tired, and sad sound.

In our time we were invited on some big and very long tours. Each time, though, we knew it would mean being on the road for three or four months. We would have sold far more records, and we might have experienced much more of the limelight, but we knew that it wasn't for us. It was a difficult decision to make. Our American record label didn't like it much, and we weren't always in agreement, but we did all settle on the fact that long tours weren't for us. God would just have to do it another way.

In time we grew to love playing in the United States. We were privileged to play in some great venues, meet many truly remarkable people, and gain some incredible insights into their lives. It was clear from the outset that these songs, which had been born amongst a bunch of guys desperate to make their faith count, also connected with people in America. It wasn't just another record-label thing— another territory to pursue as part of the master plan.

But I'm getting ahead of myself.

Our first trip out to America in July 1996 wasn't quite so grand. We'd been invited to lead worship at a conference organised by some friends at the San Luis Obispo Vineyard. We were told that there would be six hundred people and that we were going to stay in a nice hotel. A week before the event, only twelve people had registered. The hotel had been ditched, and we had been given some guy's house for the weekend. Seventeen people showed up for the conference. But they were the right seventeen people. It was electrifying, and it was the beginning.

We thought we were alone in the house in San Luis Obispo and that the guy who owned it was away. There was a lovely double bed upstairs, and we let Tim take it. The trouble was, the guy wasn't away, and he certainly wasn't expecting to find an English keyboard player sleeping in his bed when he returned home late one night and climbed into bed. *We laughed a lot that night.* Except for Tim. And the guy.

After the conference we headed south to play at the Anaheim Vineyard, the same place where I'd met Kevin Prosch a few years earlier. The power cut out halfway through the worship session, but it became another amazing experience. Just like with the thread-bare crowd up in San Luis Obispo, God showed His presence in the room.

We still buzzed from the trip when we got home. We buzzed even more when we found out a week later that Tim's idea of leaving a couple of hundred cassettes in the local church shop had been a touch of genius. They sold out quickly, and we saw again Tim's business savvy. We sent another couple of hundred tapes, and they sold just as fast. It was the start of our relationship with California—and to this day it's a special place where Delirious? has always received great support.

During those early days when there wasn't enough money to pay for a hotel, we stayed with friends, promoters, or whoever else would give us a bed. This arrangement made for some interesting experiences. Once we played at a British university's Christian union. We stayed in the student house and realised that the sheets hadn't been washed for months. *Things* were attached to them—the sort of things that really were better flushed down the toilet.

Then there was a time we played in Wales. The guy who had offered to put up Jon and Stew took them back to his house and started showing them his gun collection just before bedtime. Jon stayed awake all night, fully clothed, sitting in a chair, petrified by the notion that he was about to be massacred by a gun-wielding maniac.

But slowly things opened up for us.

When we returned home after that first trip to America we knew that we'd be back. America felt like the next obvious step, and even though the UK's an amazing country to play in, there's a ceiling you hit when you've done all the conferences and the big meetings. And we'd been doing the conferences and the big meetings for a couple years by that time. Since we'd gone full-time, we'd fallen into the rhythm of heading out on the road to play on Thursday, Friday, and Saturday, getting back home for church on Sunday with a day off on Monday, ready to deal with business in the middle of the week. It was a manic pace, and we knew it would only be so long until we had to make changes to be sustainable.

Our first big event in the United States was Creation East in 1998. We walked out onto the stage and saw eighty thousand people staring back. We all felt a little stunned. It was a long, long way from the school hall in Littlehampton and from the home church in which we'd lead worship as soon as we got home to England.

One simple but massive question hit me as I stood on that stage: *How on earth do you do this? How do you get eighty thousand people to put down the hot dogs, ditch the chatter, and listen to the noise you make? And how do you get them to do more than just listen and have a good time; how do you get them to make the active decision to join you in worshipping God Almighty?*

I didn't have any answers that day. And on that stage I wasn't much of a front man. Instead I was just a guy desperate to see the presence of God on that field. I might have been worshipping, but I wasn't really leading.

Getting your head down and ploughing on with worship was not the culture in America. I still think that the crowds in the United States are much more limber when it comes to being led: They expect the person onstage to take control and do a show even if it's one full of God-songs. I've always said that the United States taught us how to play on those big stages and opened our eyes to a new way of engaging with an audience. We came offstage at that first Creation gig knowing that we had to up our game if we were going to play more "shows" like that. It was obvious that we had a long way to go before we could present what we did to a field full of people, and I can still remember feeling utterly petrified by not knowing how to do it.

Somewhere amid that fear was something else—the sense that this could all end by being something profoundly great. I'd always thought that the two parts of me—one liked to perform, and one liked to worship—existed in separate spaces, finding different outlets. But up on a stage with a crowd that stretched out in front of us like a lake, it was different. Perhaps those two parts of me weren't strangers after all. What would it be like if I could learn how to draw the crowd in and then step aside to join them in worship? I'd never seen anyone do that in that context, but I was sure it was possible. It would just take time to get it right, particularly if that time was spent in America.

Back home we went through a frantically busy period. The bookings had flooded in. Our three-gig-per-week routine was both hugely satisfying and thoroughly tiring, but it gave us a great opportunity to connect with the growing army of people who were passionately advocating a new expression of faith. All over the UK we made new friends and strengthened old ties with people who believed that we were in the middle of a massive cultural shift.

At events up and down the country, new sounds, prayers, and messages found their voice. You never knew what would happen at any particular time—people might be broken with a sense of God's compassion or angered by injustice. Others brought the sounds of the dance clubs into the church, while some looked back at history and found fresh inspiration to pray in bold ways. The 24-7 Prayer Movement began in these days, as did the Soul Survivor conferences. During this time we took the unusual step of packing up my 24-track recording machine and bringing it with us to every gig we played for three months or so. The result was our first full-length album, *Live and in the Can*; and if you listen to it from start to finish today you get a full picture of how dynamic and passionate things were back then. One highlight was the Remix conference, where Tim kicked off with a massive keyboard pad and I just started singing out words I hadn't scripted in my mind: "There is a light that shines in the darkness, there is a light, His name is Jesus.... " Then Jonny Sertin got up and read some Scripture with such force and presence that it still makes me shiver.

In this new phase of incredible busyness it was becoming harder to find or make time to be close with God. I continued to write throughout the time as well, but looking back it's possible to see what got squeezed out in those early days: a normal rhythm of life. We rode the crest of a wave, and everything happened very fast. We grew quite disciplined with time off, breaks, and holidays, but the constant demands on our time meant it was easy for me to push away serious God-time. I would change that if I could.

But all the while a movement of people grew, and we knew that we needed to be with them. This was before podcasts, Twitter, YouTube, and easy access to fresh inspiration from around the world. In the closing years of the last century you had to physically be present in certain places to get the good stuff. One weekend we'd be with the Salvation Army, then another with evangelical Catholics, and on to an Anglican event, and of course the Soul Survivor conferences. We played our songs and met the same spirit of passionate abandonment to Christ wherever we went. I've always liked the way that God worked through us without our being affiliated to one sole tribe, denomination, or movement. That simple truth kept us aware of the fact that we cannot claim to have all the answers.

10

KING OF FOOLS

We had never made a full-length album with more than ten songs, and yet our trajectory from those early Cutting Edge albums headed towards a full-length album that would stand up next to the releases we'd see in the High Street record shops. We didn't know that the album would be called *King of Fools*. And we certainly didn't know that we were about to become a band that many would look at and ask, "What on earth is a *Christian* band?"

Even though we'd recorded and released "White Ribbon Day" as a single, we were still very much a band whose compass pointed towards the church. We might have played in sports halls and community centres around the UK, but the local churches chose the venues. We went to the streets singing, but it wasn't as if we had a master plan for the next five years. All we ever knew we summed up in a line we used at the time: We were *taking it wherever it goes*.

At this point, we'd recorded "White Ribbon Day" and *Live and in the Can*, and the songs began coming with an energy all of their own. "Revival Town" was another one that seemed cowritten with every other Christian we knew in the UK, all of us sharing in the optimism of the lyrics:

We're not on our own you know
It's all around the world
'Cause this is the freedom generation
Living for revival in this time

Revival town
That's what they're calling this place now
Revival town
It'll put a smile on your face now
Revival town

Well, I've got a story to tell
About the King above all kings
You spoke for peace, hope, love, and justice
Things that we all need today
You let a broken generation
Become a dancing generation
This is revival generation

The phrase *revival generation* stuck with many people—myself included. I genuinely felt that the whole world would soon explode with the glory of God, and that this was *the moment* in however many years of human history for which we'd all been waiting.

To some extent, *I still feel exactly the same.*

We humans are locked into our temporal mode of thinking: We can only ever see time in 2-D—the *past* and *future*. But God, we know, is above and beyond all that. For Him time is different. I don't know how different, which I guess is the point. All we know is that the Bible describes God as being out of time—that He is time-*less*, that He is omnipotent and omnipresent. All in all, it's clear that He's a lot bigger and better at this whole time thing than we are, and it is precisely because I think revival might be around the corner. I don't have a problem saying that we live in extraordinary times, even if I can barely see the "extraordinary" stuff with my own eyes. I have a sense that God is just as much at work today as He's ever been, and that's enough to transform any bunch of ordinary people into a revival generation.

When I look back on those early lyrics and all that early optimism, I have a choice: I can get cynical and say it never happened as we planned and write inoffensive songs about love just to try to get into the charts. Or I can believe that God is a God of the Possible, God of the Now and the Not Yet, a God above and beyond our understanding. To me this second option is much more appealing than the first.

I'm like a lot of people I've met—I've got something in my blood that makes common sense less appealing than faith in God. Human logic and earthly wisdom pale when compared with falling in love with the Maker of heaven and earth. I want to know Jesus, love Him, follow Him, know His whisper, and recognise His shadow. If that means making a fool of myself, then so be it. Falling in love was never supposed to be a spectator sport.

"Revival Town" wasn't the only song that was hardwired to the movement. The song "History Maker" arrived about that time too, but weirdly when we gathered all the songs together we put "History Maker" right towards the back of the record. It just goes to show how much certain songs can surprise you. It's one of the songs that would become so popular, it would outlive the band entirely. Four months after Delirious? ended, "History Maker" marched its way in to claim the number-four spot on the UK singles chart—thanks to some amazingly obsessed fans who wanted to hear it played all over the radio at Easter.

As I said, we called the album *King of Fools,* and it was an incredible collection of songs. As well as these two big anthems, there were tracks like "Sanctify," which was a little different lyrically. We looked for new ways to express things, and we looked in slightly different places for the words. We included intimate songs too, such as "August 30th" (which happened to be the date of the car crash a couple of years before) and "Hands of Kindness." We'd written these songs to be played up front on a Sunday morning, but still they captured the fragility of my broken body when I'd been in the hospital. But the heart behind them all, the anthems and the laments, beat with the same passion for Jesus.

These days I get asked all the time why Delirious? made it and other bands did not. First up, that phrase *made it* needs to be handled with care. We need to be cautious when trying to marry our notions of success with God's idea of success. Would God say that Delirious? was any more successful than the pub band who never released a single but who brought truth and light into the darkness whenever they played? Does God *like* Delirious? but prefer Coldplay? Is U2 number one on His playlist? We must not confuse human success with the godly sort.

With that said, there are some pretty practical reasons why we managed to keep going for so long. We always worked hard to write the songs, refusing to put out something that wasn't the very best we could make it. This is the best advice I can give a songwriter: Keep working, don't satisfy yourself with things being good enough, but hone and craft and polish until you've got nothing left to give.

I think we managed overall to avoid putting weak songs on our albums, but we didn't always get the sequence right. As well as shunting "History Maker" to the back of *King of Fools,* we also included "Promise" on that first album. These days I think we should have held it back for *Mezzamorphis,* the album that followed. But at the time we loved it and believed it should be on the album. The song came out of hearing from a good friend about the struggles he was having in his marriage. They're still together now, which is great, but it was a difficult time for them and a reality check for me. Life moved pretty fast for Anna and me, and we had to carve out time just to do the "being in love" stuff. "Promise" was a song about choices, and I suppose it was just another way of us looking around and singing about life. I knew we wouldn't fit into a box with our writing. One minute it was "What a Friend I've Found," and the next we rolled out a tuneful pop song like "All the Way."

Just as the album was getting ready for release, we released another single. We'd written this song called "Deeper," which was nothing more than a love song to God, with a little something extra in the music. It was catchy, and we thought it might work on the radio. The buzz of hearing "Deeper" played on the Sunday evening chart countdown when it hit number twenty was incredible. It was more fuel for the fire that burned within us. We were more convinced than ever that somehow these songs were going to become anthems that would be heard all over the radio.

As if that wasn't enough, around that time we played our biggest UK gig to date in June 1997, when our friend Noel Richards hired out London's Wembley Stadium and put on a day of music and worship. Over forty-five thousand people attended, and the day became a defining moment for us. At this event there was a symbolic handover from one generation to the next. The older guys had pulled it together, but they also invited the next generation to sing the songs.

We were just about ready for that size of gig. Not fully ready, but just about. Our songs were there, as "Sanctify" and "History Maker" were big enough to work as a stadium soundtrack. Perhaps that's why it was a good day for us, or maybe it was just that we came out kicking footballs into the crowd, wearing football jerseys, and loving every minute!

Like I said before, worship leaders in the UK at the time tended to put their heads down and push in, to worship God regardless of the size of crowd around them. I remember trying something different that day. I felt as though it was okay to enjoy the moment as well as to pour out my heart to God, and I remember thinking how great the songs sounded outdoors. After that I never really ever wanted to go back inside. Roofs and walls just felt like barriers to getting the worship out. I felt nervous beforehand—we all were—but after twenty seconds it was nothing but fun. I have every admiration for Noel and Tricia Richards, who put their house on the line to make sure the event came off, and all in all, I'd say it was a great moment for the church in the UK.

Instinctively I'm a performer—not away from the stage, where I'm a bit of an introvert—but once I'm up onstage I naturally want to involve everyone, to make people feel as though we're all in it together. From the gigs with Hope Train in the pubs around Eastbourne, and the Christmas carol competition at school—as well as all those sports matches—I've always been happy to let that side of me out. At times I felt that my showman side needed to be kept separate from the worshipper, but I knew deep down that the two were brothers, not strangers. And they enriched each other: My performance had meaning when linked to worship, which in turn was able to draw more people in when delivered with confidence in front of the crowd.

This is just the way God made me. I have the utmost respect for Graham Kendrick, whom God called so clearly to write hymns, and Daniel Bedingfield, who is called to be a pop artist. I guess I'm somewhere in the middle. But all three of us share the same desire—we all just want God to come and touch people. That's what it's always been about.

King of Fools made it onto the UK album charts at thirteen, and "Promise" hit the singles charts at precisely the same spot as "Deeper," number twenty. Mainstream radio hadn't taken to us quite the way that we had hoped they might, and we wondered why. Our first publicity person pitched us heavily as the "biggest Christian band in the UK." The logic was that since we were an underground success it was only a matter of time before the rest of the world caught on. Why not be the first radio station to lead the way and play us?

It seemed like a reasonable enough idea, I suppose, but what did we know? We were just a bunch of guys from a quiet tourist town on the south coast of England. Radio stations and pop videos were a long, long way from home.

Actually, we did have a slight problem with the whole "Christian band" tag. It just seemed a bit odd to us. We would have been happier if people had got to know us as just a band—without the religious description. It was not that we were shy of our faith or ashamed, but we didn't want to be seen as using our faith to get ahead. We didn't want to be the person who walked into a room and shouted, "Hey, I'm a Christian: Everyone listen to me!" That didn't seem like the way Jesus did things.

Instead we wanted people to be drawn to the music without any labels attached. But even though that's what we wanted, we didn't really get it. Throughout our whole career we were the "Christian rock band." We resisted at first, but eventually it became clear that we just had to live with that tag. In time we learned to be proud of it too.

But the press need an angle, they need a story, and Christianity with its seemingly narrow views and poor styling made for an obvious point of entry. Amongst us we had many, many discussions about this angle. Were we a Christian band, or were we a band who happened to be Christians? Was Stew a Christian drummer or just a drummer? If we went back to our old trades, would Stu G call himself a Christian electrician? It felt like a case of "lose if you do, lose if you don't" because people on both sides had strong feelings about the description. I think that it's a matter of taking the path that you feel God's called you to walk down. There are biblical cases—such as Esther—in which revealing your identity limits your chance of having influence. She remained faithful to God, and as a result she used her influence to change history. I think we need to be more patient with our artists and musicians if that's where they feel led to go. If they don't feel that the three-point gospel message or the Sunday morning worship circuit is their journey, let's not force them to do that as a sign of their faith. There are plenty of people who can do that.

By the autumn of 1997 we took the next step on the journey and launched our own tour of the UK. We called it the D:Tour, and over two weeks we played a stack of venues up and down our homeland. We booked mainstream venues, the sort that could seat a couple thousand people, and did whatever we could to get the message out. For the first time we didn't share the stage with a preacher, and there were no lyrics projected onto a screen. It was a shift for us, but it felt right.

The trouble with feelings is that they don't tell the whole story. We broke out of the system, and on that—and our other early tours of the UK—we may have pushed it too far, too soon. One year we performed monthly Cutting Edge meetings, sharing the stage with pastors and preachers, and the next we rented out venues with bars and sweaty smoke-stained walls, putting on a show with screens, lights, and all the rest. Internally we'd already travelled that journey, but our friends in the movement had not come so far by that point.

Honestly, part of us wanted to be rock stars. I think that this may have clouded the movement a little. This desire might have got in the way. But I don't regret putting on a jester's hat and running around like an idiot—there were aspects of the performance that were five guys having a lot of fun. But I do wonder whether we changed a bit too fast. Perhaps we should have slowed down, worried less about making ourselves different, and paid more attention to bringing people with us. Sometimes we simply decided on the best route to take, instead of making sure that we followed God's best route. I have no real regrets, other than wondering what it would have been like if we took all the energy and power of those early Cutting Edge meetings and welcomed them fully into the mainstream venues. Instead we just assumed that since we were now a proper band, God would want things to look different from when we were happy amateurs.

11

NOT BACKING DOWN

If we'd left people a little behind with the D:Tour, we opened up a gulf of miles between us and the church with our second album, *Mezzamorphis*. In some people's minds, with the release of this album we went from being a band that led the saints in worship to a bunch of dangerous individuals with dubious morals. We were misunderstood, even though the sounds on the album were as brave, as fresh, and as creative as any we ever wrote.

We recorded the album in the autumn of 1998 and decided to shake things up a little. Every time we'd gone in the studio before, producer Andy Piercy helped us. He was a great guy, very much a father figure, and we learned so much from him, but we wanted to go into new territory and decided to produce the album ourselves.

Stu G and I led the process, pushing every boundary we came up against.

I think the lyrics said it all:

I'm on the mezzanine floor,
Never been here before no no
It's a lonely place

"Mezzanine Floor"

We felt as though we were caught between two worlds—literally. The church on one hand and the mainstream on the other were both appealing to us; they both had a gravity that we knew was real. We didn't want to turn our back on either world, but standing in the middle was tough. It was lonely.

Rock 'n' roll is everything
Everything to a lonely man
And never will I bow to you

I, I'm not backing down
I, I'm not backing down

"Bliss"

The mainstream music world appealed to us, we couldn't deny it. But we were determined not to give into it completely. We wanted to hold strong, to stand face-to-face and toe-to-toe with it, and we needed to remind ourselves again and again that we weren't going to back down. Why call it "Bliss"? Because that is exactly what it feels like to stand where God has called you—no matter how hard the choices become.

Take this blindfold off of me
I'm crawling, grabbing, breathing for the way I can see
Hold me, take me, run with me, I know you'll ignite
A battered flame that once was bright

"Blindfold"

We wouldn't have written words like those in the Cutting Edge days. The truth is that we missed the connections we used to have with the people movement, and at times God felt more distant than before. Seeing the right way forward became increasingly difficult.

If I go they say I'm wrong,
If I stay there'll be no song

"Mezzanine Floor"

And there we were: *caught between two worlds.* In moving away from the church gigs we encountered criticism and accusations. But if we stayed in the church world, how would the songs get beyond the church walls? If we only ever played for Christians, how could that music make its way out to the streets?

We took these songs and did the only thing that we knew would make sense with them: We shook them up as hard as possible. We brought in weird instruments like the theremin—which makes an eerie sound kind of like the one the Beach Boys used on "Good Vibrations"—as well as a brass band and plenty of strange effects pedals. I had recorded and mixed *King of Fools*, which gave that album a certain sound, but this time we wanted a little extra help. We found a secret weapon in a man named Lynn Nichols, who was an A&R man at EMI CMG. Lynn is a great creative mind who brought a new perspective. It was the first time we rented extra gear—like a tube tech compressor (sorry if that means nothing to you, but to the techheads out there it's a beautiful bit of a kit). The whole record went through this magic box! Lynn taught me about recording different drum sounds. It was his idea to record the drums on "Blindfold" through a Baby Talk Monitor system. (Okay, sorry again—but it's another strange use of domestic gear that made us smile a lot.)

A guy called Tedd T helped create a bigger soundscape, but by far the most radical thing we did for *Mezzamorphis* was to get Jack Joseph Puig from Los Angeles to mix the album. At the time he was the man, mixing everyone from the Goo Goo Dolls and the Foo Fighters to U2 and Green Day. We took a big financial risk and paid a huge sum money for him to mix the record. It was a lot of money, but we felt that the bar was that high. We had Virgin Records on board, and they were ready to get it out to the mainstream market. We felt sure that some songs on the album could go on to become worldwide hits—such as "It's OK" and "Bliss."

We still had the same old debates: Were we a Christian band or a band of Christians? The clearest way I can express my thoughts on this now is to say this: If someone's been gifted to get up and sing a song about love that makes people cry, then that's what they should be doing. That person should be confident in their calling, and for those of us who believe in the creator God who makes and shares only good things, we should be thankful. If God chooses to put this person in a secular music environment where those songs can affect a huge range of people, those of us in the church should be forgiving, patient, and trusting.

But it's a two-way street.

The artist needs to remain connected to a gathering of local believers in some form: They need to be part of a church. They can't just charge off, disconnect themselves from the practice of community, and expect to be understood, supported, and championed by the wider church. If I'm honest, this church connection is also vital for the artist's own sanity, peace, and relationship with God. Once you get ripped out of the sort of relationships that are found in church—the sort of relationships that will ask the hard questions and keep you real, honest, and humble—you're on really dangerous ground. And if, from a position outside the church they've just left, an artist then starts criticising the church for being boring … well, this is a story we've seen many times before, and it always ends in tears.

This applies to all of us, whether we are musicians, doctors, or stay-at-home mums. If you have a heart after God you need to be held accountable and stay connected, and you'll want to remain close to friends and leaders who can keep you in check. It's a two-way street, and that's the only way it works.

So how was I doing at this point in our journey? I'd like to say that I lived in a spiritual bubble of praying every day, going to God each morning, reminding myself of the need to serve, and holding on lightly to all that was around me. But it wasn't always like that. I had a lot of ambition, I was passionate, and I wanted it.

You look back at characters in the Bible, and there's always this fusion of flesh and spirit—and we are no different. We never did anything silly, but at that point perhaps we got too hung up on the idea of being a big rock band, rather than the leaders of a movement, and there was a shift right there. I wonder whether it was at that point that the movement backed away from us—or if they felt we'd backed away from them. All that stuff about mezzanine floors—how could they sing those lyrics in church?

One line really stood out and made people mad, particularly in America:

She's as pretty as hell, and her eyes have no home
The beauty has run from your face

"It's OK"

It turned out that it was most definitely not okay to sing about anyone being "as pretty as hell," and we paid for it. We ran into big problems with one of the major chain of bookstores in America who refused to stock the album on principle. For me it was good poetry, and it described as best I could someone we had met who had just tried to commit suicide. We were somewhere in Texas on a tour and met a girl when she wandered into the café where we were eating. She opened up and told us all about how she had tried to take her own life but how something had held her back. Some of our music had helped her, and she was starting to get her life back together. But she looked terrible. She looked like she'd been to the brink of death and only just escaped. She looked as "pretty as hell."

It's a line stolen straight from *The Catcher in the Rye*—but it was too early for us to bring that to the market. It annoyed me at the time, and I had to write a paragraph in the American CD inlay explaining why we'd written it. I think the whole experience hurt us and taught us that in the United States, people can turn on you fast.

Looking back at the album now, I think there's plenty for people to get into, particularly songs like "Jesus' Blood" and "Isn't He Beautiful?" But even though you can hear the same sort of love, affection, and devotion to Jesus in those songs as in the earlier ones, we had chosen to present the album in a harder, more progressive way. We weren't doing it to annoy people or to antagonise anyone. It was simply where our creative minds were at that point.

These days I'm not so sure that particular line was wrong. I like it even more today. But I do know that we were confident back then, feeling invincible, feeling as though we could crash through any barrier in our way. We were going to be the ones to storm America, and albums like *Mezzamorphis* would chart the course.

It turns out that *Mezzamorphis* wasn't to be the great crossover album that we'd hoped. It got some good reviews in the mainstream press, but after the initial controversy, it just sort of settled down. Looking back I don't think it really had that much of a negative impact on the journey of planting music into the soil of American churches, despite the fear coming over us at the time. I'll admit that the poor sales hurt us—and we'll come to the consequences of that in the next chapter—but in time the bigger church scene forgave us for pushing the boundaries.

I wouldn't do it any differently. It was where we were back then, and we wanted to write songs that communicated to people that we all needed to be on the inside *and* the outside of church. A couple of radio stations over here in the UK played some of the songs and loved them, and we got good press from the serious UK music publications. We were still on the mezzanine floor, and it was a place that a Christian band had not visited before.

So *Mezzamorphis* was the start of our quest to make new sounds in order to communicate ancient truths to new people. It was the first of a trilogy of albums that saw us looking around, trying to work out how to be ourselves.

Artistically and creatively that album set the bar high. I still meet people today, often musicians in the United States, who say that the album was a shock to the system, which changed things for people or raised the bar a little for others. Sometimes you have to do this, to unlock something for others. And after all, do sales really matter that much?

With our heads and hearts leading us towards more creative expression, we found ourselves in a strange world. I'll always remember a meeting with the president of Virgin Records, spending ten minutes sharing my heart about the future and vision of our music. He seemed completely nonplussed, stood up, and shouted, "Well maybe we should all get out our acoustic guitars and sing ******* Kumbaya!" This was bizarre, new territory, but Virgin promised to help distribute our music into the mainstream. They would put it out, promote it, and get behind it.

But it's a fickle world. When the president of the company—the guy who happened to like what we did—moved on, his successors downgraded us on their priority list. Almost as quickly as doors began to open up, *they closed.* We still felt that we belonged in the mainstream, and we knew beyond doubt that the message belonged there—so why not the music?

That "why" was a big question for us. As time went by we began to see that there were more reasons why it would be difficult for us to make it on a global mainstream stage. In addition to the challenge of making good music and having the right connections in the right places, there was also the amount of work and money that was required. This was an era where to take a song to radio in the United States could cost around one million dollars, with no guarantees. So labels had to be sure—*really sure*—that they would get a return. Bands had to be surefire bets, and people always had their doubts about us. The fact that we only ever wanted to be away for ten days at a time scared our labels. Perhaps the fact that we began doing international gigs hurt us too—not just in the UK but South Africa, Australia, and New Zealand as well. And at the end of the day, despite all the things we said about it, from the outside looking in, we were still a completely Christian band.

For this whole thing to go off the way we had hoped and dreamed that it would, God would have to use some different blueprints than we'd expected.

But of course our destination was different from what we thought. We never did get the sort of mainstream breakthrough we had been hungry for. God had other plans for us. *Better plans.* It took a while for all this to become clear. Before the release of *Mezzamorphis* we felt sure that it would be the album to take us to the next level, and of all the albums we released it fared best with the mainstream music press.

Were we disappointed? Well, yes, and no. We had always known that whatever skills we had, these were only ever going to play a minor role in this story: Ultimately, it was up to God. So any disappointment we felt was only ever a minor concern. What mattered more at the time was finding out what God wanted and then working out the right path to take and the right songs to sing. After all, that was much more exciting than allowing some label executives to make the decisions, hoping they might take it upon themselves to support us.

Like the song said:

Rock 'n' roll is everything
Everything to a lonely man
And never will I bow to you

12

GLORIOUS

As the dust began to settle after *Mezzamorphis,* we got worried. We had not managed to take the mainstream ground that we had hoped we would with the album, but we were also fully aware of the fact that we had opened up a pretty wide gap between us and many others in the church. We were now well and truly on the mezzanine floor, halfway between two very different worlds. The idea of being able to be in both at the same time—which had seemed like such a great plan just a couple of years prior—now was harder than ever.

I think we panicked.

New conversations started to take root amongst us as a band. Could we survive without our church base? Did we need to repair that damage? How could we get them back?

It was the first time we had these type of conversations, and there was plenty of reason to have them. We had sold lots of copies of our earlier albums, but globally *Mezzamorphis* performed rather poorly at the till. As a result we had less money in the bank, and for once the future seemed less bright than it had all along. If we carried on this way, making albums that tested people's loyalty, we might not be able to do this much longer.

We asked ourselves what we were doing wrong. Today I'm not so sure that this was the right question to ask, as it gets bound up in all sorts of weird ideas, which suggest that good sales equal godly success. I don't agree with that at all. We should have been asking ourselves what we were doing right. Considering the fact that most of us were still in our twenties, it's not surprising that we weren't quite as wise as we could have been. And we were a team, taking decisions together, rising and falling together with the consequences.

As a result of our discussions, we released two albums: *Glo* in 2000 and *Audio Lessonover?* in 2001. *Glo* was our attempt to reconnect with our church base again, and *Audio Lessonover?* (called *Touch* in the United States) was a reaction to feeling a little uncomfortable wedging ourselves back into the role of "Christian band singing for the church."

Glo—short for *glorious*—is a good album. It features some great songs, like "Investigate," "Hang on to You," "Intimate Stranger," "Glorious," and "God's Romance." That album started after we worked with a producer called George Shilling on a couple of tracks but then decided to change direction in favour of making a more church-friendly record.

Even though we're proud of *Glo,* it doesn't take a genius to see the tension in the album. We brought in lots of sounds that were odd pairings—like a choir of monks and guys playing bagpipes. And, for the first time in our history, we put pictures of ourselves on the cover. It was obvious that even though this album was in some ways very much like our early music (with spontaneous breaks between the songs just like we'd included on *Live and in the Can*), we were not completely comfortable with stepping into the past.

There are many parts of *Glo* that I love. Tedd T produced the album, and then we brought in an engineer named Charles Zwicky. We recorded in a big room in an old converted church studio in Brighton, and I loved the experience. The room was full of great noises, great tones, great drum sounds, and Stu G's skills as a guitarist took off even further. We also had the opportunity to form a choir out of Delirious? fans, bringing them into the studio for an evening. There were forty or fifty people, and they sung their hearts out on songs that told of God's glory, over and over again.

The days of playing gigs up and down the UK, seeing the same faces from month to month, hearing their stories, and sharing in their joys and pains were gone. While we were happy to stay in hotels rather than spare rooms, it did mean that we spent less time sharing life, having late-night chats and breakfast conversations with the people who liked our music.

Also, to some extent, the movement itself was changing—at least in the UK. The midnineties were a unique time when evangelical Christians from a huge range of backgrounds came together to explore. By the time the millennium was over, that unity started to fragment, and people went back to doing things a little more in their own tribes again. We'd left the party to pursue things in other countries, and when we came back, we found that the party had broken up.

The stories behind *Glo* are some of my favourites. Like the time when Stu G and I were in a guitar shop and he picked up this weird old American guitar called a Dobro. It was older than his mum, and the very first sound that came out of it was the riff to "Investigate"—a beautiful, cascading little thing that has all the power of a hurricane. There was no way that he was walking out of that shop without it.

Even though we'd decided to make a "church album," we still felt that we needed to move forward creatively. You can't keep on giving people the same old thing, no matter how much some say that it is what they want. Just like with *Mezzamorphis,* we lived in the tension of knowing that if we pushed things creatively, we ran the risk of leaving the church confused and unimpressed. Yet if we brought out another album full of the same old stuff, we'd suffocate.

Today there are some worship artists doing well, but when you buy their latest album you don't expect any difference from the previous three. This doesn't seem to do justice to the awesome creative power of almighty God. Serving up the same old, same old is never on the menu for God. Why should it be okay for us?

Of course, creativity freaks some people out. The UK cover for *Glo* is a classic case in point. It became controversial with the fans, but we had a lot of fun putting together the photo shoot, which was five guys not taking themselves too seriously. We called in a stylist who liked to test the boundaries. We ended up using images of us wearing pink and yellow suits—which some people called our Teletubbies phase. But, believe me, those were the conservative shots. There's a whole set of photographs somewhere of us wearing wetsuits, and others with us wearing brown pullovers that had been all scorched and burned. Our faces were dirtied up with soot, looking like we'd just escaped from a house fire!

Using stylists was odd—although not always as odd as this. We'd got a distribution deal with Virgin in the United States, and they were keen that we do what we could to make us look a little bit better. It was the first time that anyone had taken us shopping, which was weird for our wives when we got home. *Who is this woman in the United States buying you clothes?* they'd ask. *Anyway, I like that funny old jumper that you wear.*

In time we developed our own perspective on the image of the band. We thought it was fun, and it all came under the heading "There Are No Rules." There was a bit of me that loved it all—I loved dressing up in stupid costumes. It was a part of my character.

I remember being onstage in the United States wearing a massive pair of sailor's trousers, a hooped vest that was so tight it was hard to breathe, and a feather boa around my neck, all ready to lead a worship event. Our sound engineer, Paul Burton, took one look at me and told me that I was a fool for walking about looking like an ostrich, but honestly, it felt fine at the time. God didn't seem to be telling us to tone it down, and strangely nobody criticised us for it. It was hilarious and quite possibly stupid. But that summed us up! According to our fans in America we were just eccentric Englishmen. They were very gracious to us!

What mattered more was the fact that the presence of God was tangible, and in some unusual places.

Around this time we started to improve at leading worship with big festival crowds. I learned a lot from just doing it long enough, but some things I picked up from some unorthodox sources. We toured the UK supporting Bon Jovi once, and then again with Bryan Adams, and I learned many things watching them. Seeing Jon Bon Jovi in action was a great experience, and I learned some tricks, which is an odd thing to write when you're thinking about worship. Yet it was clear that he was a genius at making everyone feel like they were with him. He'd get people to put their hands up, get them all waving together and acting as one. Instead of saying, "Thanks for coming," he'd say, "It's great that you're all here, each and every one. We're in this together, you're in the band, not just watching a show." If I could use what I learned to help bring people into a deeper shared worship experience, then that was good enough for me. I was never a big Bon Jovi fan, but I saw on that tour why their songs worked in big arenas: The songs had big melodies—driving songs that were easy to sing. The shows sometimes felt like our worship times on a Sunday morning, the crowd raising their hands in the air, wanting to be a part of something bigger than themselves.

Those support gigs were a big deal for us. We'd go out there onstage in front of a stadium of eighty thousand people and try to get them in the mood. It was a daunting task, but there was a massive sense amongst us that this was a God-opportunity.

Onstage we became a better band. In Stu G we had one of the best guitarists in the world. His tone, his sounds, his technical ability, and his emotion combined to make him absolutely irreplaceable. His sound defined Delirious?, and he was completely dedicated to his craft.

Stew Smith never really believed that he was a great drummer, and I think he always felt that he wasn't quite good enough. But he was perfect for us. He had an amazing way of making the whole drum kit move as one. Listen again to the end of "Thank You for Saving Me" or "Shaken Up," and you can hear this amazing shuffle that he creates. Once we started using Pro Tools in the studio we could see his drum patterns on the screen, each beat plotted on a grid. The weird thing was that his kick drum would always hit early while his snare would hit late—only by a millisecond, but enough to register with the software as being slightly out of time. Technically it didn't make sense, but when you close your eyes and listen, it works perfectly. Live onstage he was passionate and surely the best performer out of the lot of us. He was always exciting to watch—especially once he started competing in triathlons and grew incredibly fit. Once that happened he became a drumming machine, becoming more comfortable in his skin. He also had that sixth sense, and he seemed to know what I was going to do next.

In some ways Jon never completely relished being onstage, what with his being a quiet, introspective soul. At first he'd stand at the side to blend into the background. Soon he grew into it and became completely comfortable in his role, and night after night he held down the bottom end and kept everything rolling. He has a clever mind and always thinks out of the box, often suggesting alternative ways of doing things. The bass line on "Majesty" or the part at the end of "Mezzanine Floor"—adding in some 3/4 bars to mess up the 4/4 sections—are vintage Jon Thatcher moments.

Tim brought amazing atmospheric keyboard sounds, like his trademark sound on "Mountains," and would always bring the right mood for the song, but his true forte was playing real, authentic, old-fashioned piano. You see it best at home or at church, and he's very good. Had we the ability and the budget to transport a grand piano around, Tim would have loved it, but in reality he wove electronic sounds around the big Stu G wall of sound, which wasn't always easy. But he was gracious and kind throughout, always focused on the bigger picture. In the studio he had the ability to hear things clearly, to know when a song was good or not, early on. He would feel things in a different way than the other guys, always asking whether this was song that could carry the presence of God, beyond just sounding cool—and I appreciated that.

Before a show, we'd be doing different things in the dressing room. Stew would crack jokes and try to make me smile, warming up with his practice drum pad strapped to his knee. I'd be quiet, and from an hour beforehand my head would already be out onstage. I'd think about getting out there, what I would say, how the night would flow together. Jon would be quiet too. But you knew that, in addition to practicing his golf swing, this was what Stu G was made to do. He loved the idea that he was about to go out and unleash some epic sounds to blow people away. Tim would check email, make calls, and be developing a ten-year plan, even as we stood side stage waiting to go on. We are all so different, but this made it great.

If any one of us had a bad night, Stu G would take it the worst. On the very, very rare occasion that he had a bad gig, he'd feel awful afterwards, not that we could have heard the difference onstage.

Around 2004 or 2005 I had a bad patch. I started to lose my voice when we were on tour, so I went to see David Grant, a vocal coach with whom we'd worked on *Glo*. He took me back to basics and had me start again with my breathing and support. In the transition I did lots of shows where I was horribly out of tune. For about a year I suffered from a crisis of confidence, and some of the TV shows we did were highly embarrassing. Eventually the problem ironed itself out, but not until after I spent a long time feeling frustrated with myself.

Towards one of the last Bon Jovi gigs we had a scare. It was a Saturday night, and we'd been at my sister's wedding in the morning. We had to get a couple of hundred miles north—*and quickly*—so the only way to travel was via chartered helicopter. We felt pretty cool climbing aboard and heading off at lunchtime to play with rock stars. As seems typical of God, He had other plans, and we ran out of fuel a few miles away from the venue. We landed in a field and made our way to the stadium. It got tight, and the stress level was high. With a useless helicopter sitting in a field somewhere we thought we were stuck—about to miss the biggest gig of our lives. But somehow the police helped us out. We got a lift with them, rammed in the back of the sort of van they use to round up the drunk guys at the end of a football match. We sped into the venue eight minutes late to see Bon Jovi watching us from backstage as we piled out of the van, ran onstage, and kicked off our first song. We felt pretty good.

Having seen *Mezzamorphis* come and go, the gigs with Bon Jovi felt like another kind of launch pad—and so did the ones with Bryan Adams. We'd been lacking in confidence, wondering whether we could play with the big boys, but these two tours encouraged us. Others might disagree, but we knew that we could go on those big stages, face a crowd that didn't know us, play our songs, and feel confident that those could connect with people. It was tempting to think that the Christian label was a barrier, but I honestly don't think that it was. We had a sense that we walked in God's calling, and we loved it. I felt alive up there, and I knew that this was where we were meant to be. It's true that we weren't singing overt lyrics like "I've found Jesus," but in our hearts and minds we were living out the words "open up the doors and let the music play."

Those moments of certainty helped us through the hard times when others accused us of losing it or giving up. I can understand how they reached those conclusions, but the truth was far from that. We made hard decisions to keep going in spite of other people's disappointments, and I know that God's presence at times felt tangible. In these moments, I felt like every part of my body was alive and awake in new ways. There was blood flowing, faith rising—and I expected God to come in power in those places. During one set on the Bryan Adams tour we played "Investigate," and I said in the middle, "Right, let's all lift our hands to heaven." I watched as the ocean of people in front of me did just that. Then I said one of those prayers that you pray with every ounce of your being:

"Let the fire come!"

I think that at that point I knew a little of what Esther in the Bible had to go through, keeping her identity secret but trusting God for everything. I don't know who God touched, what miracles happened, but I know that I prayed the prayer and wanted to stand in the gap for the crowd. I remember watching Stew playing like a man possessed, pounding out healing drum tones that filled the skies. It was as though he was in the centre of the crowd, calling people to God with every whack of his snare. We believed in all that crazy stuff, that one hit of a floor tom could show God's presence, and we

believed it even more in a field with thousands of Bryan Adams fans
who needed a touch of God.

There was a time when a friend of ours died. Chris Blair was a
famous mastering engineer at Abbey Road who had worked on some
of the greatest albums from bands such as Radiohead, Coldplay, and
Sting. He seemed to like our stuff and had asked that I sing "Every
Little Thing" at his funeral.

I was honoured. The church that day was full of music-industry
people and a handful of celebrities. I knew that for those three and
a half minutes I would have people's ears, and in a strange way it
felt just like that first time when I had stood up in front of my peers
at school. I felt nervous but confident in God. It was one of those
moments I knew God had engineered, and it was my responsibility
to be a voice of hope in that situation.

Away from the tours, however, there were disappointments.
People would tell us that they couldn't sing our new songs. They
were right. There was a general feeling we heard from fans that we
were no longer giving people what they wanted. That made us sad,
particularly as I believe that there was always a prophetic side to
our songs. I don't mean this in an arrogant way, but when you lead
a group of people, sometimes there are moments when you can't
give them what they want. To keep people growing you have to go
beyond. I know that sounds a bit arrogant, but it's true.

From the outside it probably looked like we morphed and
changed, that we outgrew some of the earlier stuff. Internally we
never wandered too far from the days of playing in the school hall.
Through the whole time we were never away from home longer than
ten days at a time, we always tried to put family and kids first, and we

still led worship at church once a month. The whole time we played together as a band we all remained members of the same church—the one run by my father-in-law. It kept us more grounded, more stable than we might otherwise have become. And there was a degree of security that came from being known at our home church and not being able to hide behind a costume or a stage.

However, because I wear my heart on my sleeve, I tended to come back from trips—and the studio—with a bit of me missing. I'm particularly intense and focused in the studio and not very present when I return home in the evening. My mind's often still full of music and tunes, and I can be very hard to live with at those times. Leaving my studio, Planet Music, can be hard for me. It's very frustrating for Anna when she needs me to be hands-on, and some days I'm good at it, and other days I'm not.

Each of us in the band, to a greater or lesser extent, did most of our transition into adulthood while we were in the band. But like any transition, there are good days and bad days, some decisions that are better than others. Sometimes our failings were public, just like any of the things we got right.

I'm glad of that. Had we only ever presented an image of perfection it would have been wrong. Not only would it have been incorrect, but it would have meant that we were hiding the truth. As it was, we chose to display all the mess and mistakes for all to see. Our odd-looking photo shoots, our attempts to play the game of part-time rock stars, and the lyrics that left some annoyed were always completely public.

Having said that, when I look back to some of the lyrics, the spirit of Cutting Edge is in there:

I'm gazing at the sun, keeps me younger now I'm older
But we've only just begun, feel Your hand upon my shoulder.
Sing it loud, all we need is fire and a cloud.
Your love, it is the compass of my heart.
Your love, it is the thing that let me start.

There can be no doubt that we had the compass in our hands, that our love of Jesus was strong. But our future direction was uncertain.

Too often as Christians we have an allergic reaction to failure. Perhaps it's because we associate it with the big falls from grace that grab the headlines; perhaps we have some twisted guilt that results in our feeling as though we let God down. Whatever the reason, it is never healthy to try to sweep our mess under the carpet. It never works.

13

ROLLERCOASTER

They say that creative people make the worst businesspeople. All that passion and desire to come up with something new doesn't always work on the bottom line. Having pushed *Glo* out to the church, it was time for us to complete the second step of our two-step plan and release another mainstream album. Only this time, we wanted to do something bigger, bolder, and more "businesslike" than ever.

To us, the logic was so simple. We were locked into a distribution deal with EMI in the United States, which meant that we owned our records but EMI still pushed them out through their pipeline. We felt convinced that we could do it better. Or, if not better, we could at least do it as well as they could, plus tailor the system to suit us. The fact of the matter was that many people who bought our albums went to church, yet they weren't necessarily the sorts of people who spent a lot of time shopping in Christian stores. We wondered if we could connect with them directly. It was that same old invincible spirit, only this time it was about to really cost us.

Sometimes when you're a part of a bigger label, that label's energy and loyalty are spread over twenty artists, which can be frustrating. We liked the idea of having our own label, of having someone wake up every day thinking about what they could do to help get our next album—*Audio Lessonover?/Touch*—out to a wider audience. We had set up our own record label in the UK way back when, and it served us well. The scene is so small in the UK that Furious Records UK was a small operation. But what if we launched Furious Records in the United States and still partnered with EMI on distribution? Couldn't we come out with a far better deal?

In order to set up Furious Records USA we needed to employ someone full time in Nashville, gather other artists on our roster, offer advances, and start releasing albums for those other artists. However, the venture had compromises, and within a year it was clear that the project was not going to work. By the time it folded we'd lost a six-figure sum of money.

It hurt us badly, and for the first time in this adventure we were on the back foot. The atmosphere changed around the band and management, shifting from offence to defence. After this one failed venture we went from being a band searching for our next calling, to a business with debts that needed to be paid. Up to that point we had a sense that God had given us ideas and we'd had the resources to run with them. But not now. We entered new territory, shaving money off here and there, cutting budgets, and taking wage cuts. It was the first financially negative experience we'd gone through, and none of us liked it one bit.

I have no regrets, though. After all, it's only money. But I do feel sad about the fact that subtly we became less dangerous and less adventurous. As I said before, we were a team, and we made decisions together, and therefore we were all responsible. But just maybe we forgot that our primary focus was not to run a record label in America but to lead people into the presence of God. We could have owned our own tour bus, PA system, or even set up our own festival—all these possibilities came up at various points during our journey—but wisdom comes in knowing God's calling for you.

With Tony Patoto on board and five strong personalities in the band, we were an incredibly strong team. Because of this we could develop plans and deliver strategies ourselves, without much help from the outside. For the most part, this created incredible energy and a feeling of invincibility, but the downside was the fact that we had a bit of a siege mentality. On some occasions several people offered opinions or questioned what we did with the business, and at times we didn't listen enough. To my own shame I would often miss the clarity, wisdom, and common sense that Anna brought.

Some of the problem derived from our lack of experience, and some of it was the fact that *Audio Lessonover?/Touch* was not the strongest record to launch a label. Again, we were a team in both the highs and the lows, and it wasn't the time for pointing the finger at each other. We had to press on, learn from the experience, and humble ourselves amongst our contemporaries and—even more importantly—humble ourselves before God.

Perhaps that's the root of it all: We tried to drive this new business, not let God.

If *Glo* was our teenage phase, then it was that silly sort of fourteen-year-old time. *Audio Lessonover?/Touch* was Delirious? as that sulky, moody seventeen-year-old, the sort who takes the car out and returns it stinking of cigarettes and empty of fuel. All I can say for sure is that we tried to find something to say but had a hard, hard time coming up with any real sense of God's direction.

This time was made harder by the fact that recording the album was difficult. We had an engineer who wasn't sympathetic to our cause, and perhaps he worked against us at certain points. I think we had something to communicate, but we hadn't found the way to articulate it. We feared getting stuck in a box or being perceived as boring and felt scared of being moulded by American Christian radio. *Audio Lessonover?/Touch* featured some brilliant moments, containing some of our most creative work to date. But the album lacked an overall unity. It was awkward in its own skin, and the tension in the studio with the producer didn't help. Stu G did not enjoy the experience of being sidelined by flutes and oboes, which for a guitarist of his skill is perfectly understandable. Stu and I were used to driving all the production decisions, but we felt more distant in that role on this record.

Of course, as ever, Stu G came alive in the studio, in spite of the influx of classical instruments. He took a whole leap forward, adding a certain strangeness to the sound. When I listen to tracks like "Rollercoaster," "Stealing Time," "America," and "Angel in Disguise" I think we hit something. But starting with "Waiting for the Summer" didn't work, and releasing it as a single was worse. It just wasn't who we were. It was an attempt at a throwaway pop song, and we put it out as a single because radio people told us that it was the best thing that we had, but in our world it never worked. For us *Audio Lessonover?/Touch* is even more personal than *Mezzamorphis*, even more full of questions and lines with *I, me,* or *my.*

At this point we moved more into a traditional rock-band phase, renting venues and playing shows in secular venues, but this was mainly in the UK and occasional gigs in America. However, the vast majority of the time we played songs such as "Deeper," "Mountains," and "I Could Sing of Your Love Forever." Whenever we got on a plane we'd wind the clocks back five years, as most of the churches who invited us to play wanted to hear those songs. I liked that sense of difference, even though at times it felt a little schizophrenic.

When we were on duty as a mainstream rock band, we started to actually see why we were there. I think that we were good at making friends with people, and we made it a priority to be courteous to those with whom we came into contact. There would be preconceived ideas of who and what we would be like, but when we met up with presenters or directors, cameramen or journalists, things always went well. In the mainstream world people just couldn't get their heads around how to play the music on the radio, how they could play songs genuinely about God there. I can understand that. Our songs are about things that were unfamiliar in that world. God hadn't been on the charts for a while.

I remember us doing an interview with *Q*—the UK's leading music magazine. After the piece was published, I wrote to the journalist to thank him for his time. Apparently it was the first time that had happened. Another time I gave my lunatic red, flowery trousers to a TV presenter up in Glasgow. It wasn't a big deal, but years later I saw her again and she remembered it. She remembered this strange Christian band in the studio, and she remembered that we talked about our kids and staying married, and yes, she remembered the Gucci flowered trousers.

We did some fun gigs—like playing with the band Muse in New York City, or sharing the stage with Feeder or Matchbox Twenty. These shows were exciting, even though the reality was far less glamorous than it sounds. We enjoyed having someone validate the music. After all that's what you crave as a band: the sound of people hearing your music and liking it. As a Christian band, however, you live in a strange place: The music is less important than the "ministry" or the message, and after a while you start to wonder whether you really are any good as a songwriter. Are people just buying the records because they feel like it's an expression of their faith, that it's a part of their duty, or do they actually like the music over which you're sweating?

There were a couple of times we got tracks played on mainstream national radio, and I liked the feeling I got as I heard the songs start up. But once I heard "Deeper" played after a Spice Girls track I realised that it's not really pop music that we made. We were heading somewhere else entirely.

Back in those early days, when I travelled around the Christian conferences and festivals, I got to see Christian leaders and artists without their masks on, which was eye opening. Years later as we flew around the world and stayed in nice hotels I also met some mainstream rock stars without their masks on. We'd meet them at after-show parties or industry events and made a lot of friends in those places. People just doing their best to get through and be faithful to their music.

At times the Christian scene is more dangerous. Sometimes, we have this Disneyland existence where we all have to pretend to be squeaky clean, yet reality's not like that. Sometimes things are happening in secret that are not healthy: alcohol problems, pornography, people travelling too much or getting into trouble, but it all gets covered up even though it exists, behind closed doors with the "Do Not Disturb" signs dangling on the outside. If I was hanging out at a mainstream party, I might not agree with what a certain singer of a certain secular band was up to, but at least what you saw was what you got. This sort of honesty was endearing.

Seeing that world up close—a world that many of us in the church would write off as sinful or beyond the covering of God's grace—was and is a privilege. And at times it left me more than a little bit scared. I remember going to a Virgin Records party while we mixed *Mezzamorphis* in LA, and around midnight a bag of cocaine surfaced. I was a kid with a sheltered Christian upbringing—never smoked, never been drunk, always done the right thing—and suddenly, there was all this powder. I'd never seen anything like it, and I was amazed how much everyone suddenly woke up! It was a long way from the Littlehampton school hall, but we still knew we were on the same mission to see God use us wherever we ended up.

In the times when we join people in their daily lives we can make stronger connections. It's the same reason that so much of the New Testament was played out on the streets, in marketplaces, or within the homes of those in need. Sure, there are scenes that take place in the temple, but Christianity works best when it's shared beyond the walls of the church. And the really great thing is that it works in all places, because love, sacrifice, acceptance, hope, and healing are needed everywhere. If you look past the "sin" you find people with good hearts who want to do better but who just don't quite know how great it is to come home to Jesus.

I'm fortunate that my parents provided me with a strong moral and spiritual framework. Many of these others I met had not had the benefit of that sort of upbringing. Are they beyond God's grace? Could He not reach the places they live? It strikes me that Jesus spent so much of His time with those who had baggage, issues, or hangovers. Are we so sure that doing likewise is off the menu for us?

But living in that tension can be hard. One day we were leading a few thousand singing "I Could Sing of Your Love Forever," with hands raised high and hearts on fire for Jesus; the next week we could be surrounded by people who had never been near a church, whose lives were a mess, and whose morality was questionable. Saints and sinners, we played for them all. And I honestly think that it was right. I truly believe that God put us in those places, and it was a privilege to serve people, regardless of their faith. But we had to be on our guard to the traps in both camps: Pride is no respecter of location, and both saints and sinners can appeal to your ego.

Plenty of great Christians in the music industry right now are living their faith out loud. We must stand with them and cheer them on. There is a crazy new wave of God music coming through that will be difficult for people *not* to listen to; it's the spirit of being "louder than the radio."

I think we're heading for a time when the walls between Christian and secular music will come down. Christian music needs the innovation and the ability to make music without religious constraints on creativity, while the mainstream world is desperate for music that connects people to something bigger than themselves, ultimately to God.

There were other symptoms of the tension of this double life. The UK tours had always been the one opportunity where we could assume both sides of the band at once. We'd put on these grand tours with rock-and-roll lights, costume changes, and all the rest, and fill the venues with our own church fans, many of whom brought their bemused friends. But with the songs from *Audio Lessonover?/Touch* we soon realised that if we played all twelve of the new ones we left people a little dissatisfied. We constantly felt the need to delve back into our church-song catalogue. You can never get away from the favourite songs that became soundtracks for people's lives, but we always lived in this musical tension, which we tried to navigate with a gratefulness that people still loved to see us live.

We seemed to run into more resistance in the United States. We had to rerelease *Audio Lessonover?*, calling it *Touch*, redoing the order completely, remixing a couple of songs, and taking a couple off. We added in a new title track that we had recorded a few years earlier. I didn't mind having to do that. In fact, I enjoyed the creativity of the whole process. "Love Is the Compass" returned to the original version we recorded at Ridge Farm with Mr. Shilling, which I preferred, and we learned a lesson about not straying too far ahead of people.

Yet it wasn't all happy days.

Tony Patoto stepped down from being our manager in order to move his family to Nashville—a move that we all agreed was right and good, despite the fact that we knew we would miss him like

crazy. With *Audio Lessonover?/Touch* missing the mark we got to the
end of this season and had to take stock.

Were we going to continue? Did Furious USA have a future?
What was the sound that we wanted to have? What was our calling?

14

MAJESTY

You know that saying about how one door closes as another opens? Well, just as our days as a rock band with mainstream hopes came under serious pressure, a whole other bunch of unexpected opportunities suddenly presented themselves.

Having spent much of our time on planes heading west, it pretty quickly became clear that something was going on in the east as well as the south. We started getting invites to play from all over the world: Singapore, Malaysia, South America, Russia, and Colombia, as well as New Zealand and Australia. There was even talk of China being open to the idea of a Delirious? tour, which blew our minds.

If the thought of going to these new places was exciting, that was nothing compared to what we'd find once we actually arrived. I will never forget flying into Bogotá to lead ten thousand Colombians in worship. They knew every word and sang with a passion that still leaves me breathless.

We still did serious-looking photo shoots and pushed for air-play, but gradually the balance of our effort shifted towards these new opportunities. Stepping off the plane in Rio or São Paolo was like going back in time. Suddenly we joined in with thousands of Christians crying out for God to come and move in their land. "Obsession," "Mountains," "Sanctify," "History Maker"—the songs came alive again.

It all started with Hillsong. I'd written to Darlene Zschech a while before, saying that I admired what she'd been doing and asking if we could meet up. Once we got to know each other, we ended up heading off to the Hillsong conference in Sydney. We flew in and made our way from the airport to a youth meeting that we'd been invited to play. For us the term "youth conference" meant a couple of hundred kids with acres of space around them. We couldn't have been more wrong. There were five thousand young people, ready to go, eager to worship their Saviour and Friend. We didn't have time to set up the gear so we did an acoustic "History Maker" with Stew on a set of bongos! It felt like the roof was going to come off.

Once you play at something like the Hillsong conference, you find that all these people who attended begin to send you invites to join them at their own churches. We loved the opportunities that opened up, and the chance to meet our cousins from churches around the globe changed us in ways we could have never imagined.

All around the world we connected with people, inspirational people who were passionate about their movements. In their minds it was all about opening up the doors and letting the music play, singing in the streets that Jesus is alive—and that sense of the clock being turned back thrilled us all. We could return to the early days with the benefit of experience, as well as the excitement of seeing how these expressions of worship could change lives and transform communities. It felt as if we had a glimpse into the future.

As time went by, we began to see how each location brought out a different side of us. In Rio the reactions were so immense that we played the biggest anthems we could find, I remember the first time the crowd sang so loud I couldn't hear a thing—*it was exhilarating*. Singapore was a completely different culture, so we offered up songs to reflect the heartbeat there. Colombia would be gritty, and California always felt much more like things did back home in the UK.

I was shocked to discover that just because things went a certain way in California the rest of the country didn't always follow suit. We found out that, in general, American churches were quite conservative compared to those we knew elsewhere, and it reminded me how easy it is for us in the UK to take for granted the heritage of revival and awakening that runs through our DNA.

There were other shocks in store for us as well. Our home church in Littlehampton has always met in a school hall, and we have never had many more than four hundred members and two or three members of staff. On our tours, we often turned up at church buildings that looked like the Microsoft campus, which made our jaws drop. Seeing huge buildings that included a school, a gym, a football pitch, and more was unbelievable. When we discovered that the church paid full-time worship leaders and a pastor who pulled up in a brand-new car, we knew that we were at the start of yet another sharp learning curve.

I never want to trash this kind of church. It would be incredibly arrogant of me to judge them. All I knew was that, whenever I found myself at the start of one of these new experience curves, I needed to stop, ask questions, listen, and pray. Every time I began one of these learning journeys I saw something of God that inspired me. And I loved finding out new things about the way the church looked in different cultures. Of course there were things that I saw that I would not copy and paste over into my own life, but I never considered that as giving me permission to snub another person's faith.

I will make one comment about big churches: After a while it became obvious that many of them are quite territorial, and that's true whether you're in Singapore, South Africa, or South Carolina. I still find it sad to drive past three or four huge churches and find out that they don't speak to each other. You never know the full story, but whether the disagreements are about theology or about brands of coffee, it strikes me that there is a better way forward. Unity transcends time, style, and numbers. When people hold hands across their own theologies, that unity can bring down the modern-day walls of Jericho.

Of course, if you're an average church in the UK that employs just a couple of people and is, for all intents and purposes, just a slightly boosted cell group or small group, then snubbing your neighbours and going it alone simply isn't an option. So in this sense, perhaps there's something good about "small," too.

Hillsong Australia was one of those big churches that taught us plenty. Mark and Darlene Zschech inspired me—the way he served his wife and particularly the way she acted with her team. They'd constantly be helping one another, handing over the position of leadership with grace and generosity. And when they led worship it was like nothing I'd ever experienced before: The size of it was like a church on steroids, but even though we stood in an arena, the setting felt truly intimate. That blew me away, every time.

Over the years Anna and I grew closer to Darlene and Mark and stayed with them from time to time. We started to connect with people who were outside our Delirious? world, people like Michael W. Smith, Israel Houghton, Chris Tomlin, and Paul Baloche. I had no idea then how significant each and every one of these relationships would become, but at the time it was enough just to feel connected to a wider family.

We met someone else in those years who would play a more considerable role than we could tell at the time. His name was Greg Laurie, and he'd booked a baseball stadium in Los Angeles and invited us to play music. Greg is an evangelist who is totally focused on winning people back to Jesus, so his events were a great environment to be in. We found ourselves on more and more of these big stages, and the responsibilities increased. Maybe it was because we'd been around for a decade and people started to trust us a little more, or maybe it was because we'd reconnected with our role as the guys who provided a soundtrack to the change within the church. Maybe this had been God's plan all along.

Whatever their cause, I loved these new opportunities. New songs flooded in as a result, and Stu G was on fire. We wrote songs such as "Rain Down," "Inside Outside," and the song that would be the manifesto for the rest of our years together as a band: "Majesty."

Because of the failure of Furious Records USA we were on our knees when we wrote that song. We desperately needed God to help us, to get through some of those bumps, and there was a shared sense of our fragility. I remember Stu G had set up a studio in the corner of the office, behind some cardboard boxes. He called me over one day and played me a song.

It started with one of those Stu G guitar parts that few others ever seem to be able to come up with. Tender and honest, it looped and repeated in on itself, winding down before repeating back again from the top.

The lyrics are perfectly in sync with the riff:

Here I am, humbled by Your Majesty
Covered by Your grace so free
Here I am, knowing I'm a sinful man
Covered by the blood of the Lamb

I was in! Stu G expressed perfectly where we were. I cried. I was deeply touched by the song. The chorus came later in the studio, a soaring bird of exquisite beauty and power:

Majesty, Majesty
Your grace has found me just as I am
Empty-handed, but alive in Your hands
Majesty, Majesty
Forever I am changed by Your love
In the presence of Your Majesty

After the very first time of hearing "Majesty," I knew we had our signpost to guide us through the next phase. It put into song the feelings we shared: that we had tried all we could—tried singles, tried radio, tried putting money into videos and press. But it was time to surrender. We were full of bright ideas, but none of them was worth anything unless God came and breathed on us again. It was time for us to surrender. It was time for us to get to our knees.

I will always be grateful to Greg Laurie for the invite to that baseball stadium in Anaheim, California. Apart from our church, it was there that we played "Majesty" for the first time. Greg's team managed to get some clips of a new film that was about to come out. Few of us thought that Mel Gibson would ever make a film that would so powerfully enhance our understanding of our Lord's crucifixion, but that's exactly what *The Passion of the Christ* did. As we played our song of surrender, images of Jim Caviezel walking and suffering as Jesus filled the stadium. It was very powerful moment and, for us, the start of something new.

The church could never have made that bloody, violent film, but God used Mel Gibson powerfully. In the short term it had a massive effect—and in cinema screens all over the United States whole churches were buying up tickets. Had it been different—say, if every time the film was shown someone asked who wanted to give his or her life to Jesus—the response could have been incredible. But it wasn't to go that way.

Yet it smelt a little like revival. And we felt revived ourselves.

Eventually these new songs came together and got presented as *World Service,* our seventh full-length studio album. The title was an obvious choice, even though it wasn't shared with any of the songs on the album. We just felt convinced of two things: Things were now global, and we needed to serve.

Even though we'd had our budgets clipped by the failed label in America, we still felt as though there were no limits. The invites came in from every continent, and we made connections with amazing people. We'd never had a platinum record in the United States, like lots of our peers, and making the decision to travel far and wide was sure to mean that our support in America would only decline, *but it felt right.*

Those opportunities were the start of our hearts getting ripped out. We had been to South Africa, and some of the others in the band had spent time getting to know a project for orphans of HIV that we'd supported, but it was not until *World Service* that the reality of global poverty began to press in against our flesh.

I remember being on the beach in Rio. It's beautiful, just as the postcards suggest. But the sudden realisation hit me that one block back there was brutal poverty, trafficking, and prostitution. I couldn't relax in the sand knowing this; I couldn't rest with this knowledge gnawing at my conscience. Before this, I hadn't really considered poverty much, but somehow, now I was faced with awkward questions. *What difference was I going to make? My heart told me that injustice was wrong, but what were my head and hands going to do about it? If my love of Jesus meant anything, could I really walk away from all this, could I turn my back?*

I don't know why that time in Rio was so significant, and I can't remember exactly what caused it. I do know that I felt like I was at the start of yet another learning curve. But this was sharper and steeper than any we'd seen before. And even more exciting.

Then came the song "Rain Down." It arrived during one sound check when Stu G was playing around with a riff. It took off right then and there, and soon after we were in the studio recording the song.

Jon had become a friend of UK-based artist Daniel Bedingfield, who had just had a number-one hit with "If You're Not the One." Jon invited Daniel along to the studio on the day we recorded the vocals for "Rain Down." We met at my house, where Daniel strolled in and lay down on the sofa.

"So Martin," he said, "why haven't you had a number one yet? Do you think it's because the songs just aren't good enough?"

I knew I liked him straightaway.

When we got into the studio, the first thing Daniel did was to strip down to his boxer shorts and socks. I still have no idea why he did this, but he seemed to be the kind of guy who it was best just to allow a little "freedom." He jumped in the vocal booth with us, and we started singing the chorus. It was Friday afternoon, and these group vocals weren't all that urgent. We wanted to nail the take and then get home to get the kids fed and in the bath. Whatever we didn't finish then we could do on Monday. But Daniel was intense, and this wasn't good enough for him.

"Stop!" he shouted midway through the first take. "Guys, I'm the only one here that's worshipping."

Fair enough, we shrugged.

But it was Friday, and it was just a backing vocal that didn't really matter. Did we have to push it that hard?

"Yes, we do. So let's worship!"

We started singing again, and out of the corner of my eye I could see Jon lifting up his arm. Before long we were all at it, singing to

God, and Daniel was happy. There we were, our hands in the air, Daniel in his underpants.

Strange but memorable.

But maybe that story is more than just a funny little anecdote. Perhaps it's a reminder of how we need to keep worshipping. Perhaps it shows how we were too caught up in the busyness of things to allow God to break in. Perhaps it's a reminder of how God caught our hearts again. All I know for sure is that by the time *World Service* came out, we were back.

15

100 MILLION FACES STARING AT THE SKY

It's funny how love affairs start. Something captures your heart, and often someone helps bring you together.

Joyce Meyer was our Cupid when we fell in love with India.

We'd never met Joyce, but one day we got a call from the Joyce Meyer Ministries office to say that they would like us to be a part of an event in the United States. Anna and I had watched some of Joyce's programmes on TV every now and again. I thought it was interesting, even though I didn't quite understand the big American preacher thing. I thought it was a little bit glitzy on the presentation, but I couldn't fault the content. So it was a no-brainer: I wanted to go and get to know this intriguing lady.

I remember feeling really nervous, more nervous about meeting

Joyce Meyer than I'd been about meeting Jon Bon Jovi. It felt like quite an honour to play on her stage, and I guess we must have done an okay job, because the invites to take part in more gigs with Joyce followed. Most of these were in America, but there were some further afield. On these trips the lights suddenly went on for us. We discovered a little of who Joyce is and how she ticks and saw this incredible family doing incredible things, giving millions of dollars away to save people's lives across the planet. Thanks to them, there are better-funded schools, hospitals, and orphanages in countries that desperately need them. Even though stylistically, I wasn't used to their events, it was obvious that God was up to something, and I loved every chance we got to be a part.

Again something bigger was going on. In the old days I'd see people onstage and then be less sure about some of them when I got to know them in person. But with Joyce the process worked the other way: Any questions I had after seeing the programmes vanished once I met her and saw her in action. I've known Joyce for a few years now, and I can say that with her what you see is truly what you get. My life is better for witnessing her commitment to making her faith count.

As I said, India was the place where our hearts broke. We'd played a gig in some nice-looking London venue a few days before, so arriving in Hyderabad made for a massive culture shock. You land at the airport, and there are thousands of people, and there's chaos and electricity about the place. Everyone is working, but there doesn't seem to be anyone in charge. It doesn't smell good, and there are beggars everywhere. People run and shout all around you, all while two hundred cars wedge into a car park designed for fifty. The first time it feels like landing on the moon. I loved it and hated it all at once.

We arrived to play at one of Joyce's massive outdoor conferences. It was exhilarating, and all the more exciting as we knew that nobody would have a clue who we were. Honestly, for this little worship rock band from Littlehampton, playing in front of four hundred thousand people was the most significant night of our lives.

Four hundred thousand people is a big crowd.

We couldn't see the end of the crowd, and there was an energy present that was truly awe-inspiring. The majority of these people were not used to the culture of what we were doing, and thousands upon thousands had probably walked fifteen miles from their villages and brought their granny and their food for the day, as well as their cow.

I remembered then, the words the man had prophesied for me years before, on the night before I wrote "Did You Feel the Mountains Tremble?" He had told me that "one day you'll play in India, and when you pick up your guitar mountains are going to tremble." In all my years of playing, that one night was the ultimate moment for me. All the pieces of my life came together, and I felt as alive as I ever have been. It made those Bon Jovi gigs pale by comparison, and my head was full of the simple thought that this was why I'd been born.

The beautiful presence of God was obvious there. For a time the old barriers of class, caste, and language vanished, and the character and presence of Jesus was incredibly powerful. It was a visual representation of the gospel: the doctors and the beggars, the wealthy and the poor, with Jesus in the middle of it all, saying, "This is okay. I'm comfortable with all of this."

We went to a few other cities on that trip and saw some of the orphanages and feeding projects that Joyce Meyer Ministries funds.

We got our hands dirty, and in a matter of minutes, I tried cooking up a plan to return with Anna and the kids—something I longed to do.

This wasn't the first time I'd come face-to-face with poverty. In Rio de Janeiro, Brazil, my mind started to think more about extreme poverty. And Stu G and I had seen difficult things up close when we'd visited Rwanda in 2004, a decade after the horrific genocide. Mark and Darlene Zschech had decided to do what they could to help bring hope back to that country. One thing led to another, and there was a big celebration in the stadium with the government officials all there, everyone united in praise and prayer. Together they acknowledged the hurt they shared and looked to God as the only source of hope. The fact that the people of Rwanda had suffered so much but were able to forgive was unbelievably powerful. That genocide wasn't like a horrific train crash that claimed two hundred lives: It was colossal, deliberate, systematic, and prolonged. Every area of the country was affected, and nobody escaped the grief. It was shameful, and it will take generations to process, but so many of us outsiders felt shocked by the country's ability to forgive, as well as people's ability to forgive one another individually.

To see events like this cannot help but change your perspective. It showed us that the hope we find in Jesus has very practical applications. It showed us that nations can change and that justice is worth fighting and praying for. More than anything, though, our trip to Rwanda softened our hearts in preparation for what was to come.

That process of preparing the ground went through another significant phase a year after our first trip with Joyce to Hyderabad. With a lot of help from our new friend, the amazing Scott Norling, we put on a tour of India: Hyderabad, Pune, Bangalore, and Mumbai. These were ten-thousand-people-a-night shows, all outdoors, and for us it felt like real historymaking. Not many bands had come along to India before to put on a rock show, but through the process we met more and more of those remarkable Christians who help change their world.

Of course, with all of these experiences filling up our senses we had to put them into songs and record another album. *The Mission Bell* might have been recorded in England, but it was written in our heads and hearts amongst the dust and duct tape, the noise and the people of India.

One of the longest-lasting songs to emerge was "Now Is the Time." With its random rhythm, it asks the key question that was on our minds:

I want to follow but what does it mean,
To live in this world and keep everything clean?

It was a different lyric from those that came before. It was ragged, a little dangerous, and certainly uncomfortable:

Nothing I own here is ever my own,
When I live in the mercy and blessing You've shown.
I lay down my rights; see the world through Your eyes,
And fight for the hungry who pay for our lives,
I want to have You in all of my world.
So Jesus consume me, flow through me, 'cause now is the time ...

The changes in us were real, and these words came from the deepest part of ourselves. We'd now made friends with great people who were very, very poor; we had met kids who owned less than we threw away without thinking. I saved their photos and stored them on my computer. Bit by bit, poverty became personal. I could no longer ignore these friends; I could no longer hop on a plane and simply think about the next destination.

It started to change the conversations at home. I'd bring photos and videos back and want to share the stories with the family. It wasn't always easy, but I knew that it was too important just to push it aside.

Another song on *The Mission Bell* describes the awkwardness that we felt. "Our God Reigns" became a song that challenges but connects with people. It has an unusual lyric to put in front of an average congregation, but my church family at Arun Community gravitated towards it. It was inspired by a hymn from the seventies with the same title that I sang as a kid.

> *40 million babies lost to God's great orphanage,*
> *It's a modern-day genocide and a modern-day disgrace*
> *If this is a human right then why aren't we free?*
> *The only freedom we have is in a man nailed to a tree.*

> *100 million faces, staring at the sky,*
> *Wondering if this HIV will ever pass us by.*
> *The devil stole the rain, and hope trickles down the plug,*
> *But still my Chinese takeaway could pay for someone's drugs.*

This song features some of the lyrics with which I'm most happy. It's not hard to understand, and it puts into words the lengthy conversations that we were all having.

In fact, the song grew out of a conversation in my kitchen with Matt Redman. I'd just come back from Rwanda and asked him, "Why didn't we all do something? We knew what was going on, but why did we stay silent? Why did we do nothing?"

Matt listened for a while and then replied.

"I don't know, Martin, but it's a little bit like abortion. That's like genocide, and we don't do much about it. But one day we'll look back on our postmodern society and ask how it was that we were able to murder our own children?"

Now, I know that the issue is complicated, and I certainly don't want to condemn or make it a statement of judgement. I'm not going after anyone involved in making those decisions, but I felt like it was something I ought to write about. When the current estimate is that through April 2010 (some numbers coming from as early as 1922) there have been 950,000,000 abortions worldwide,[1] something is surely not right. All I knew to say was this: "We may have lost our voice, but we have not lost our hope." The other reason I love "Our God Reigns" is because it's a lesson in singing things that are true. There are times when we may not "feel" like God reigns. We might feel that He has gone on holiday and left the planet. But the fact is—*the truth is*—whatever happens, our God reigns.

I believe that singing big statements of truth with each other helps our faith rise. When people unite and speak with one voice— or shout, scream, or whisper—things can change. If only we spoke with greater unity and clarity, politicians would be unable to ignore us. The power of gathered masses has been the key to every major

---

1 Compiled by Willam Robert Johnston, "Summary of Registered Abortions Worldwide, through April 2010," www.johnstonsarchive.net/policy/abortion/wrjp3310.html, accessed October 2010.

social change over the centuries. Put another way, if we dislike the way the world is heading, it's up to us to act wisely, boldly, and in unity with others to change it. All the individualism stuff that our culture pushes at us—the idea that "me" matters more than "we," that *my* rights trump *our* rights, that we are all our own little gods rather than servants of a great heavenly Master—*it's wrong.* We were never meant to be alone, living out our faith without connection to other believers. We're part of a team called the church, and our team has the power to turn the world upside down, if only we could relinquish more of our own territory and pride and let God take control.

Delirious? could have had five number-one hits and a big career played out on a big stage, but that would have been insignificant compared to the power of even a fraction of the church's potential. When the church gets together and the people movement finds our lungs and our hands and feet, the world waits with bated breath.

For me the release of *The Mission Bell* reintroduced a profound sense of excitement about everything. Far from feeling that the Hyderabad shows were a high that could be followed only by a sense of disappointment, it filled me with a sense of passion, energy, and purpose that I'd not experienced for a while.

16

COMPASSIONART

Parties with the music-industry suits were quite a shock. But the surprise of a few middle-aged men trying to recapture their youth through illegal drugs was nothing compared to what I felt when I met a load of impoverished children living in one of the world's largest slums. This was Dharavi in Mumbai—*Slumdog Millionaire* without the long-range forecast of a life transformed. And, more importantly, this was one of Dharavi's red-light districts, an open brothel where the children in front of me—those smiling, beautiful children with eyes like the darkest oceans—were the children of prostitutes.

These were the children who, while their mothers worked, would hide quietly under the bed or take their chances out on the streets. These were the children who grew up with a single parent whose life was defined by risk and danger. These were the children—the girls at least—who had little option in life other than to follow their mothers and become prostitutes themselves, probably even before they hit age thirteen.

That visit—the one when I met Farin—changed my life. I don't think that I would be doing what I am now, having left the band and launched CompassionArt, had it not been for that two-hour visit. I wouldn't have rediscovered something in myself that went back to my early twenties and the word *India* being spoken over me. If it hadn't been for Farin, life now would look a whole lot different.

In the months that followed that trip to Mumbai, it wasn't unusual for me to spend time thinking about the fate of those children, in particular the girls. To see a child so full of innocence, beauty, and life, and to know that unless something truly dramatic is done she will end up making a living by exposing herself to sexual abuse day in, day out, messes with your head. And the impact on your heart is not far behind.

Looking back now, it makes sense that I reacted as I did. There has always been that element within me, and even though my upbringing was a typical middle-class one, my parents made sure we knew what life was like beyond the world of weekend cricket and European holidays. Mum and Dad instilled in each of us a compassion for people that were less well off. We all knew how Dad—whose own father was a doctor—had enjoyed the privilege of growing up in a seven-bedroom house while my council-estate mother didn't get her first toothbrush until she was eight.

I think that idea was there in the early songs as well, the sense that we are here for God as well as to serve people. Who wanted to stay back and barricade ourselves inside the church? Poverty, injustice, and inequality are there to be tackled through actions as well as through music.

So when I arrived in India I felt in some way as though I'd come home. It was as if I'd found something for which I'd previously been looking. Part of that feeling surely derived from the prophecy that had been given to me when I was twenty-four, about trembling mountains and playing in India. In so many ways it all felt natural. Why wouldn't I be surrounded by orphans and feeding bowls and rows of beautiful, smiling children who no concept of the risks that lay ahead for them in life?

Meeting Farin and seeing her across the room was a shock. I was doubly shocked that I could be impacted so deeply by her, though I suppose in other ways it was a natural reaction. Of course, I was going to meet some child one day and want to bring him or her home. It was the sort of thing that God would do.

While meeting Farin was a crystallising moment for me, it wasn't all calm serenity and blessed assurance. My heart felt ripped out, fibre by fibre, and I was left with my head wired up to the mains by a sense of absolute emergency. I wanted to adopt her and take her out of that dangerous place as soon as possible. That sense of emergency dissipated weeks later when the local pastor called to tell us that Farin's mum was no longer keen on her daughter moving to live with us in England, and thanks to the continued brilliant work of the team there at Prem Kiran, the organisation where I met Farin, Farin's family are doing well and her future now looks far safer than it did before.

But the feelings didn't go away for me. Farin was okay, but what about the others? What about the other 1.2 million children trafficked each year? (See www.stopthetraffik.org for more information.) How many other Farins were there across the world, hiding from dangerous clients, kidnapped from their homes, or waiting for the day when they too would finally be pulled in by the gravity of dire poverty?

Was the story really over?

I think that everything worked out the right way. I know that God saved us from a wrong path, and there are changes that have taken place for me as well as for Anna. We have had to find other ways of doing what we can to engage in problems that we feel stirred about. We have had to be creative, to hold on tighter to God, to find the ways of keeping from retreating.

I had spent time thinking more and more about working with other artists. Perhaps it was inevitable after so long with the band, but as time moved on, the idea of getting others together to write a new batch of worship songs for the church became an increasingly strong idea running throughout my mind.

And at some point God breathed on it: Why not use the songs to raise money? Why not pull together the best worship songwriters I knew, work them ridiculously hard in ways that they had probably never been asked to work before, and get them to hand over any claim to copyright of the songs as a result? We could make an album, and all the proceeds could be used to fight poverty in all its forms worldwide. Would anyone be fool enough to say yes?

I didn't even get to the end of my speech with Tim Hughes before he interrupted me.

"Martin, it sounds like God. I'm in."

I was shocked and grateful. Then I had the conversation with Darlene and Mark Zschech. They felt the same. They were in too. Then Michael W. Smith, would he agree? He had no need to say yes, having already done so much good work for charity. Could I persuade him?

It turned out that I didn't have to. He said yes straightaway.

As the weeks passed by and the phone calls went out, we enlisted a growing number of people behind the aim of joining their art and compassion. The CompassionArt project was born, and we set about getting ready for the weeklong songwriting retreat that we scheduled for January 2008.

I never intended for CompassionArt to replace Delirious?. It was a side project that I planned to manage with Anna, but not one that would threaten Delirious? in any way. This was simply a moment in time when we realised we had to do something, and we told ourselves we would cope with whatever came along as a result.

Even so, we started to get a sense that something unusual was happening. Not only had we managed to coordinate the schedules of twelve very busy artists, but we had managed to get them to agree to seeing absolutely no money from the experience. And, to top it all off, their respective record labels, publishers, managers, and agents had released them and agreed to waive their usual fees. This was a development I never thought was possible, but it happened. I was stunned.

And then, as the time for the writing session approached, I started to feel overwhelmed by it all. I was nervous. What if we didn't write any songs at all? What if they weren't good enough? Would people take the risk? Would they gel in the short amount of time we had for bonding before they got down to business? Would there be any ego battles? What about the artists who were due to go into the studio—would they give away their best creative ideas, or would they hold back for their own albums?

We held a retreat in a beautiful house on Loch Tay in the Scottish highlands. My friend Jim McNeish, a good and wise man, owns the house. The setting bristled with perfection, with the water of the loch acting as a perfect mirror to the mountains that stare down on it. Add that to Jim's ability to see what makes people tick, and we couldn't have picked a better location.

As we gathered for that first evening I could tell that some of us felt nervous. The room was too quiet, and people weren't talking much. There were many people in addition to the eleven writers (Chris Tomlin was back home in the hospital fighting off an infection), including husbands, wives, and a few friends to help keep things moving along.

I get quite shy in front of groups of people. I'm fine in front of fifty thousand people, but put me in a room with a couple dozen and my mouth starts to go dry and my guts contract. That's what I felt as I drew the names from the hat and sent people off for the first writing session. I was younger than some of the others, and compared to most people I'd not had much in the way of commercial success. I've never had a platinum record, never won a Grammy or scored a big radio hit. *Were these guys really going to do what I asked and reach down into their deepest beings? Would they give their all?*

Two hours later Jim called us back in, and we sat around the piano, listening to the results of the first writing session. I knew right away that we would be okay.

As the week went on, the songs that came back into the room were strong—stronger than I'd hoped. It was obvious that people had let their guards down, and that early hope of writing songs that would save lives became even more of a certainty.

By the end of the week we'd gone from being a collection of individuals to feeling like a true team. From mealtimes to writing sessions, from worshipping together to learning more about Scripture and God's heart for the poor, there was a sweet presence of God throughout the week.

Everyone brought their best, and with great characters like Israel—a man who is such a force of nature—in the mix, that early nervousness soon disappeared. Darlene, who processes everything with a worshipful mind-set, often closed her eyes to see if she could feel the Holy Spirit, while Graham Kendrick obsessed about the lyrics, making sure that every word was theologically correct. He'd be up late at night, working on the words, while Stu G, Paul Baloche, and others would be sitting around the fire making new connections and asking the hard questions.

It felt like a move of God. I know it's not two hundred thousand people getting healed, but there was something miraculous about that time. The songs that emerged are still owned entirely by the CompassionArt Trust, and any money they generate is used to fight poverty around the world.

I've spoken to plenty of musicians who were inspired by the songs and further impacted by the fact that we'd given all the money away. Both the Christian and the mainstream music industries looked on and were a little shocked. Typically when musicians respond to charity it takes the form of a day in the studio recording a single or a trip overseas with media in tow to raise awareness. While those efforts are great, it's a credit to the writers who joined CompassionArt that they gave away so much.

———

Where are we today?

Well, so far the songs have generated less than the millions of dollars I'd secretly dreamed about. It's more like tens of thousands of dollars rather than larger figures. I've learned to listen to God saying, "Don't judge it by human criteria." Was it successful? Yes. Twelve people who could have kept their ideas and songs back for themselves decided to give. They showed up, let their hearts be stirred, and left empty-handed. CompassionArt was successful because we ran with the plan.

People have asked whether I've been disappointed, whether it was a lot of fuss over nothing, even whether it was a mistake. I wonder whether I let God down, whether I messed up, whether it should have been different, whether I should have done more.

I think we probably went too far with some things. In my industry head, having spent nearly twenty years making records, perhaps a bit of me got in the way. In the aftermath of it all, we have handed the CompassionArt name over to Compassion International, the child sponsorship organisation. The vision and passion is still there, but we will have to rebrand at some stage if we want to rebuild for the future. We know that at some point God could touch the songs, have someone cover any one of them, and the income would increase. They're there for God to touch, not for Anna and me to worry about.

So what's my verdict on CompassionArt? I'm happy that we've given away a certain amount of money that has provided relief, health care, and hope for people around the world. But there's something else I am excited about: the fact that some of those relationships between the writers have grown in wonderful ways. Michael W. Smith and Steven Curtis Chapman have now toured together, and since we let down our guard and discovered that we're better together than as separately orbiting individuals, there's been a massive shift in the writing process.

Look at the songwriting credits on new albums from Matt, Darlene, Tim, or others, and many of the songs are now collaborative. I'm beginning to think that the days of individuals writing worship songs might be over.

17

GOOD TO GREAT

Anna and I devoted three years of our life to the CompassionArt project. Did it cost us? Yes, it did, but not as much as it would have if God had not been involved. That sense of walking on the right path, and of being in step with our Father in heaven, transforms even the hardest tasks, doesn't it?

While we both knew God was in that project, in these days since the project has completed, we've been left asking some hard questions.

Was it all just a great story? Doesn't it look as though I got a lot of mileage out of it, as if I came out nicely? I spoke a lot about Farin, but she's not living with us. Do I really care?

I know that I was deeply moved, more profoundly than at any point on this whole Delirious? journey. I still feel like I am in some way responsible for Farin and her family. I don't know what the future holds, but I know that I am connected to her. But I don't think that those big questions deserve just a single paragraph of an answer. They need more space to breathe.

I need to tell you that at times I feel like a bit of a fake. I'm obviously not selling all my possessions and giving them to the poor. I must therefore be a fraud. Either I'm really doing this or I'm not. Either I really care or I don't. You can't half care, can you? At times, I know that I'm more excited about watching an England football match than about all the good I could do out there.

This has been a battle within my soul. I have had to continually return to what I feel it is that God has called me to do. Previously I would have thought that meant I was doing something wrong, but when it comes to compassion, I reckon that the awkward, nagging feelings are a sign you're on the right track.

When it comes to compassion, the black-and-white way of thinking doesn't seem to work so well. *Do we really think there is such a thing as having* enough *compassion? Can we have* enough *generosity?*

Of course not. But it's hard to get out of the guilty mind-set.

I think about the real heroes of our faith, the ones living it out today. Some of these people have chosen to live amongst the poor when they could well have chosen otherwise. These heroes help build God's kingdom in the places where it is desperately needed. But God's kingdom needs building all over, amongst the wealthy as well as the poor, amongst those who make the policies as well as those who deliver them. Can you say that living amongst the poor is a more significant role than being prime minister or president, than being a teacher, a pastor, or a singer in a movement? I don't know.

But I do know this: You have to stick to your calling and be true to the thing God created you to do. We are part of one body.

But even so, there's a deep sense that the words of Jesus about giving our lives away are pointed right at me. I haven't given my life away; I've kept quite a lot of it back for myself. This is the daily tussle of my soul. *Am I a fake? Do I really mean all this?* I've had to say, "God, I can't figure it out; if You tell me to do something I'll do it." So these days the challenge has become less about the good stuff I can do and more about the extent to which I can listen to God and hear His instructions.

Sometimes the tension is painful for me. A few years back I installed a recording studio in my house, and I needed to spend a lot of money to make it happen. I knew that the amount could pay for ten members of staff at Prem Kiran or even go a long way to open a medical centre. Could I really justify spending all that money?

I remember God saying to me: "But what have I asked you to do? What have I given you permission for? Isn't it to make music that will touch the planet?"

That idea of permission feels like the right way forward. I'm looking to Him for permission to do things, trying to listen to the Holy Spirit. If there's permission to take the kids to the movies or on a holiday, then I'll celebrate that. If there's permission to put cash towards spending time amongst those living in poverty, then I'll do that and celebrate it.

In some ways it requires a certain type of bravery to hold on to your sense of calling when that calling has you stuck in the middle of this consumer culture. You're probably like me—called to live out your faith in your workplace or neighbourhood, in the supermarket and the gym. Jesus is not absent from those places, and His Spirit is constantly active, ready to draw your attention to the people He wants to touch. How exciting and accessible is that?

At some point when I was raising money to record the CompassionArt album, someone I was asking frowned and said: "Why should I give you money? Your writers are all successful and wealthy. Why can't they put their hands in their pockets?"

I saw his point, but I think he was wrong. When we make decisions on our own giving based on what we think other people are—or are not—doing, it seems to me like we're on the wrong track. Giving must be a response to the Spirit, not a calculated judgement on what we can or cannot get away with.

I've got friends who are wealthy and who have transformed entire communities with their generosity. And I know others who are poor because they've chosen to give as much as they could. Both respond to the calling, both make their decisions on what God tells them, not what others think.

I find it hard to maintain the energy I might have at the times when my compassion gets spiked. Living in a Western society with Starbucks down the road and High Street stores ramming out great deals all the time, it's easy to forget. I forget. I can't maintain the pace, and I certainly don't wake every morning, saying, "How am I going to fight injustice today?" Most mornings my head is full of sounds of kids wanting breakfast and melodies that might make it into songs.

Thankfully some people do wake up asking that—but I'm not one of them. The important thing is to figure out that thing God has called you to do. For me that's writing songs and creating a space where people can experience the presence of God. It's singing into the darkness and hearing people's hearts break.

So, yes, I could abandon that and put all my energies into a big push for malaria aid, but I wouldn't be very good at it. I've met people who are born to do that, the sort of people who wake up in the morning ready, willing, and excited to get to the bottom of injustice. They're far, far better at it than I am.

However, sticking to what you're called to doesn't mean you turn your back on injustice. Thankfully, over the last five years we in the church throughout the world appear to have woken up to the cries of those around us. I think there's been a huge prophetic push from God, saying, "How can you say you love Me when you live this way?" It feels as though we are learning again what it means to be Christians.

—

Writing this now, we are a few months on from the devastating earthquake in Haiti. We learned a lot about ourselves as a result of the crisis that followed the earthquake. We saw people giving all they could, we saw Haiti turn to God in prayer, and we discovered how hope can emerge from the rubble with arms outstretched.

I learned some things too. I learned that the human soul doesn't have the capacity to respond to all the suffering that we see in pictures. In the same week that Haiti was devastated by an earthquake, a good friend from church here in our village died suddenly. I just didn't have the emotional capacity to fully engage with both.

Having seen poverty firsthand I was disappointed with my response. Shouldn't I have been saving the day? Shouldn't my faith have pushed me out? Shouldn't I have boarded the next flight to Port-au-Prince—or returned to the slums of Mumbai, for that matter?

None of us can do everything, but at times it feels as though I'm doing almost nothing. Just meeting my family's needs in my role as a husband and father feels like an incredible challenge. But I know that I'm needed here at home right now. For the moment I need to be a better husband and father.

I do know the way God works with me; He makes things personal. Before India, I never once woke up in the middle of the night worrying about the plight of those caught up in the sex trade. But once I'd stood face-to-face with Farin it was different. She went from being one step removed from me to being a daughter. "She's precious to Me" was all I could hear from God, and I knew something had changed within me.

God doesn't see statistics or issues. He sees people. He sees His children.

And that includes children like you and me.

———

It was a privilege to hold the microphone for Delirious? and rally the troops, but there were times when it was hard. Sometimes your heart is heavy and your head is troubled—and going out onstage to lead a crowd in worshipful celebration of our God and King feels like the last thing you want to do.

At those times I felt that God understood. I've read enough of my Bible to know that life isn't perfect and that up onstage I am not always going to be floating on the perfect spiritual cloud. And you can't always trust your own emotions—I might come offstage and think it had been amazing, whereas Stu might feel blank. Next night I might come off feeling like I'd not connected, like everything I'd said was rubbish, but Jon might say, "No way! I was watching this kid all night, and he was crying and God was obviously moving in his life—what a great night!"

You learn quickly that you can't trust your own emotions; you can't adjudicate it, because you're not the one to judge how it went.

But then again at times emotions do tell something of what's going on. You cannot live on this planet without getting hurt, and you can't experience a relationship without the highs and the lows. I completely adore and love my wife, yet there are moments when we hurt each other. I don't know why it happens, but it does. Being in a band and travelling the world puts a certain strain on a relationship, and at times we spent more time apart than together. Most of the time our relationship has been amazing, but we've had our stresses as well. There were hard decisions made that hurt others, and there were times when those wounds and that feeling of being misunderstood and hurt came with me onto the stage. On the few occasions that happened I knew that by the time I got to the mic I had to dump all that baggage. I couldn't bring that junk onto a stage and then ask people to love God with all their hearts.

The hardest shows of all were in 2004. Most years we toured the United States at Easter with all our families. Anna was pregnant with our fifth child, but she started bleeding the morning that we were due to leave home. Everything within me wanted to cancel the tour, but we couldn't. Anna and I spent the whole flight with her losing that baby, and when we arrived in the United States, I just wanted to go home. But there was a three-week tour for us to do. I didn't want to carry on.

The other guys carried me. I remember I collapsed into Jon's arms one night before going back on for the encore. He carried me. *Literally.*

———

All those years ago when I was at ICC recording Bible-week seminars, I saw preachers with their families backstage. It helped me to form ideas about what sort of husband and father I wanted to be. For example, I knew for sure that if I was going to have a family I wouldn't want them to be a distant additional benefit that had to fall in line with the ministry.

Our first daughter, Elle, came along, and life instantly became very different for us. I was a novice, but Anna was trained as a nursery nurse and showed me how to do everything being a father required. I've tried to be hands-on, to come back from wherever I've been and be as present as possible. Elle's always been quite nurturing, so I had a gentle introduction to being a father. Then came Noah, a completely different character. He's a true alpha male, into sports and drumming, and he already thinks he's a rock star. He has a tender spirit, too, and loves being part of a big family. Indi is cerebral—a deep thinker who communicates constantly by writing little notes. She's very headstrong, and we call her our Justice Fighter. There's no grey with Indi. Levi is Noah's opposite: He wants to care for people, asks lots and lots of questions, and loves cars and anything that moves. I've learned to share his passions. Then there's Ruby, who is a bit removed from things and is often in her own space. She has so much of me in her. I always ask her whether she's seen any angels that day, and she giggles. She changes her clothes three times each day, and nothing ever matches, but that's Ruby. Mary, our youngest, could almost be Ruby's older sister. She's big, bold, stocky, brash, in control, always bossing the whole family about, and a lot of fun. It's too early to know what she's going to be like, but whatever happens, she'll try to get her way.

Having so many kids keeps you humble. How? Well, you never feel like you're winning. You can never feel as though you could write a parenting book as there's always some challenge stirring up somewhere in the house. There's usually one more bedtime story to read or more football to play, and we often need God to help.

But these children have enriched my life. I have a tendency to be more introspective and like my own space to process things, but they pull me out of my head and into a house full of friends, movie nights, football, or any number of any other events. They've saved me from being too serious and introduced me to a new side of God's character that I didn't understand before: the fact that He is fun.

When I heard God say that my time with the band was over, my six children played a large part in the decision. In particular, my relationship with Noah made it clear that stepping down from the band was the right thing to do. He was ten at the time, and we were at a critical point in his life. There was a slight feeling of disconnection between us, and I knew that he wanted me around more. It wasn't complicated. I just needed to be home. They all just needed their dad. They needed their dad to show that he loved and valued their mum, too, and that family came first.

18

THE FIVE-STAR DREAM

Dear Martin,
I love what you do. How can I have a career as a worship leader like you too?
Yours truly,

———

I get this sort of email a lot these days. It troubles me a little.

Worship leading as a career choice? To me this is a completely alien concept. The thought that you can strategise and plan and wage a campaign to become someone who helps other Christians enter into the presence of God, somehow seems wrong. Admittedly in countries like the United States, where there are so many more churches that have the money to employ their worship leaders, it might be possible to sketch out a few plans for how to use your gifts, but I still don't think that it's right to see worship leading as a "career." Those emails still bother me.

However, I love what is going on with Worship Central, Tim Hughes' training centre at Holy Trinity Brompton in London, where they are training worship leaders in every aspect. They're far less concerned with what goes on onstage than the formation of a character of integrity. Leading worship might lead to a career, but that's the result of a heart devoted to leading people into God's presence. Too often we can get confused between the journey and the destination, thinking that ending up onstage or with an album is a sign that we have "made it." Some of the greatest worship leaders I've met—men and women with humility, anointing, and a beautiful relationship with Jesus—are unknown outside their own churches. Are they any less successful? No way.

As a band we didn't set out to model how a church worship band should look. We were five white middle-class men playing as some kind of glorified folk band. We were never trying to set ourselves up as the Sunday-morning model for people to follow, and that's why those emails trouble me. We don't need a whole lot of Delirious? clones. The church is crying out for an army of people committed to being themselves, to expressing and leading their communities in worship, whether in the slums of Mumbai or at the three-hundred-year-old organ at Holy Trinity Brompton. The key is being faithful in what God's calls you to do. Faithfulness is more eternally powerful than ability.

I didn't plan on doing this. I didn't have a strategy for worship. It was entirely a God-thing. Hopefully I've been true to the story, true to the way that it happened so much by God's hand rather than by my own skills.

———

Today things are different. Right now there's a framework in place around worship, a machine made up of publishers, management, labels, and copyright-licensing bodies. There are ways to make money and increase that cash flow. The machine now generates its own inertia, its own traction, and it preserves itself.

Worship has become an industry in and of itself. Perhaps I'm overstating this a little, but this view isn't exactly uncommon.

Could we do without the machine? It depends what you call it. If you rename it a support mechanism, then I think it can help. Some of the most amazing, godly, Spirit-filled men and women are working to help give resources to the church's worship today. They want to see God's glory reflected in our nations. But others are less so, others perhaps don't care so much about worship and instead are building a brand or strengthening an empire. We need more of the keepers of the vision, more of the men and women who hold the standards up high, more of the ones who can hold on to the primary reason for this thing that some of us call God-music—that it's here to touch people, and when it does, lives change.

At times I feel as though I have seen too much: too many air-plane meals on plastic trays; too many beggars on the way back to the hotel; too many Christian bands suffering from an imposed blueprint.

You're a worship leader at your church. You write songs and serve alongside your community. People have probably known you for years, seen you grow up, watched as you've shared in the lifeblood of the local church. They've heard your songs and taken them on as anthems of their own. After all, that's what they are, since the worship that you lead them in comes from all of you.

The songs start to get attention, and a record label signs you. You go on tour for 250 days a year, and if things go well between you and your band you'll stay together that first year. But at the end of the tour you realise that even though you've played in two hundred churches, you've not been to church for twelve months. You've lost your connections with the people who shaped you, with your community, and you're disconnected.

You feel the need to write songs again, but instead of the songs pouring out from the shared experiences of your faith community, you start to write about the things that you think you *ought to be* singing about. Within three or four years you are so far from the original reason you started writing and leading worship that you're in danger of burning out—or worse, doing something really stupid. But maybe that wouldn't be so bad after all. If you could just tear down the facade, wouldn't it all just get better?

On more than one occasion I've seen bands and artists follow that path.

How can bands avoid it? We need wise counsel, strong community, and the courage to accept that there's more to life than serving the sales agenda. If you're married, then maybe you can't be away for more than a hundred days a year. If you have kids, maybe that number ought to be lower, or maybe you work out a way so that you can all travel together. If you're faced with the chance to take the career to the next level, do these costs come into the equation?

I love the story of God telling Moses to go back and command Pharaoh to set His people free. Moses knew that the only way it could work was if God went with him.

Only if God goes with us.

How's that for a guide to making those big decisions? Forget the profit or the profile—why not just ask God and see if He's in it?

I've not seen enough decisions made this way, and I've not made enough decisions this way either. But if we get better at going to God instead of charging on alone, don't you think the world would be a better place? Couldn't this be the clearest signpost to transformation?

———

Some time after the CompassionArt project was recorded, Delirious? went on the road again with a new album to play. We wrote *Kingdom of Comfort* with our heads messed up by poverty and full of the deep confusion that comes from visiting slums in India while sleeping in a five-star hotel.

Like the song "Love Will Find a Way" says:

I stare in the eyes of this flesh and bone
I'm a tourist here so tomorrow I go home

I try to make sense of the things I've seen
Between the poverty and the five-star dream.

We were messed up, in a very good way. The album's title track said it all too:

I built myself a happy home
In my palace on my own
My castle falling in the sand
Pull me out, please grab my hand
I just forgot where I came from

Save me save me
From the kingdom of comfort where I am king
From my unhealthy lust of material things

Those words "save me" are delivered with feeling. Real feeling. Standing onstage, knowing that my house was just as wealthy and comfortable as it had been before I went to India and having my heart ripped out—it was real.

I suppose I was careful to ask questions rather than make statements about people. I struggled with these issues, aware of the fact that I'd come a long way from Acts 2 with its radical community of Christians prepared to give whatever they could to advance the kingdom.

The album created more questions, more dialogue, and more tension amongst the band. Our tour of India had just ended, and the very first thing that had happened upon our return was this: Stu G wheeled his amps into the studio, set them up, and unleashed the most dirty, angry, and painful chord I've ever heard. It's hard to explain if you're not a musician, but in that chord was India—all the sorrow, frustration, and anger with ourselves for doing so little, and all the hope that it could be so different. In it I could hear something different.

I think we got some elements of that sound on the album. And I think that was right. After all, we still hadn't got the whole poverty-justice thing tied up neatly in our own lives.

That was abundantly clear in the summer of 2007 when we took all our families to Asia. My kids got to meet Farin and experience what life was like for children living on a rubbish dump in Cambodia. But we also enjoyed great times in Singapore and Bali. It was schizophrenic but okay. We wanted to connect our kids to a deep sense of responsibility, to broaden their minds, and to show them how different life is for most people on this planet. It wasn't an attempt to stop them from asking for a PlayStation or a new pair of shoes; rather, it was our way of sharing with them a little of what can go on when I leave the house. Meeting Farin was an important part of this, and certainly a seed has been sown in our eldest four children that life is bigger than we might otherwise think.

Amongst all the confusion and the questions of the last few years came some real points of clarity, such as the fact that once you meet Jesus you can't ever really be the same. Once you meet Him and understand that He died for the whole world, you can't shut yourself behind the gates. We live in a small world, and we have to be aware of both our global and our local responsibilities.

I also know that you've got to know your God. You've got to know His voice and be confident in what He's saying to you. With that in place, who cares if life is lacking in comfort?

———

Looking back I wonder whether we should have ended when Stew left. Then again I wonder whether things changed when Tony left. We carried on for five years after Tony left. And those five years might not have been the most comfortable, but our eyes opened in ways we'd never experienced before. Perhaps it wasn't such a bad call.

People always ask me about the end of Delirious?. Did the relationships break down? Did things go wrong? What failed? Was there something sinister beneath the surface that brought us down? I think what happened to us was what happens to a lot of teams who grow up together. I felt that we'd simply reached the end of the journey together and knew that the next stages would be travelled in different directions. I knew I'd completed that assignment.

For me the decision was made in discussion with Anna. We both felt like we had completed that particular assignment. We both felt like we were done. That was all there was to it. Others in the band wanted to do other things, and Stew Smith had already ended his time as our drummer and moved on to pursue his amazing gifts as a graphic designer and creative director. But it was more than the logic that convinced me of the decision. I had a sense that just as God had been there at the start of it all, He was also there at the end of that.

When the time came to tell the band, I felt peaceful. But it was odd to ask them to be released from the band when the month before, we'd been looking at how the next decade might pan out for us. I can understand that for the guys it may have looked as though I was coming up with some crazy idea on a whim. But it was a decision Anna and I made together, prayed about, and sensed God at the heart of it.

After that there was an eighteen-month period where we made plans to dismantle the band and the business, sell the gear, stop taking bookings, and take ourselves out for a final tour. It was a hard time for all of us. We knew that journey was over, yet there were still many months left to work through. There were times when all I wanted to do was leave my passport at home, show up at the airport, and pretend to be shocked at the revelation that I was therefore unable to travel. I never did that, by the way. But I wanted to. *More than once.*

It wasn't easy for the rest of the guys either. The news that I wanted them to release me from the band was a shock. In some way, it threw their futures up into the air and left them to work out how they would continue. That was a process that each of them went through individually, navigating how the future would look. And, of course, what with most of us related to each other by marriage, this was a decision that affected so many relationships and families.

Eventually the months passed, and we got ready to go onstage for our final show. Some of the pain had subsided, and we were ready to play with the same passion and sense of purpose that had fired us up for seventeen years. Stu G, Jon, Tim, and Evans had been on a difficult journey, but I'm proud that we made it through to that point together. Any ending is difficult, particularly the end of something that worked so well and became a community—*a family*—for us for so long. But it was "the lowering of a flag" as a friend said, "ready for each person to put new colours on."

We'd called it the Farewell Show and had taken over one of those nice-looking venues in London that we all loved. I was nervous. It had been a long eighteen months, and our exits from the band had all been carried out at different speeds. And of all the shows we'd ever done—from those early worship experiences in school halls to the ones where the stage was dwarfed by hundreds of thousands underneath the electric Indian sky, this one was the one in which I felt the most pressure.

One side of me wanted to suck every ounce of life out of the gigs, knowing that this was the only time in my life I would get to celebrate the journey that Delirious? travelled. But the other half of me felt so responsible for the filming. I couldn't mumble or fumble my words, and it had to be a great show. I think you can see both sides of my brain working on the final DVD.

The show went well, and it felt as though it was the right way to end. Someone told me that he thought it was an occasion to be treated with a little respect and reverence. I can see that.

But what I loved most about the night was that we ended with the song that closed our very last album. Ten years before we ended the band, someone said that, like King David when he was a shepherd boy, our first song was a simple song of love to God. "My Soul Sings" is exactly that, the sort of song to sing when you've run out of words. When there are no more big or important things to say, when there's nothing clever or wise or insightful left, all you have is the sound of a group of shepherd boys just saying it as simply as possible. It's a love song, and I couldn't think of a better way to close out the final minutes in the life of Delirious?.

In many ways it's the perfect final song. It's Cutting Edge through and through: simple, passionate, and true. We ended where we began, singing about how great God is. It seems right to conclude that way.

People used to talk about a good death, and for us, this was it.

———

This chapter started out with a few comments about the state of the worship industry today. I suppose it might have come across as though I've become cynical. I'm not. I'm full of wild hope. If you talk to the right people you'll see signs of change taking place. Listen carefully enough, and you can hear new songs coming through—songs that come as the result of people learning what it means to get to know Jesus. In my songwriting today, I'm writing less about how to save the world, more about "have you seen how amazing He is, my Lover?" Intimacy is my priority as God once again draws me back to understand what it means to love and be loved by our heavenly Father.

Maybe it's just me, but I find that change really exciting.

19

KEEP THE FAITH

It's been eight months since I knelt in front of our last ever Delirious? crowd, the tears falling down my face as five thousand people sang, "My soul sings, my soul sings, my soul sings—*how I love You.*" It was quite a night.

Life is much different for me right now. I've been at home for nearly every one of the past twenty-six Saturdays, and I can now cook decent chicken fajitas. My wife tells me that I'm a far nicer person to be around.

Yes, I'm in transition, on a journey to something new without knowing what it is or where it is or how long it will take to get there. But I do know that a strange thing is happening to me—I'm discovering an amazing commodity. It's called "space." Space revealed a world to me that I forgot existed. Time to walk, read, fall in love again, and spend minutes, not just seconds, gazing upon my children's faces as they sleep. I've nothing against the one-hundred-mph worship sets and the challenge of cramming nineteen songs into twenty-two minutes, but I feel a new thing coming, at least for me.

Space is as important as content, and silence as important as singing. Our music and art should be filled with more beauty, more grace, and definitely more space. In the layer beneath the text God speaks to us; in the silence we hear God's heartbeat; and without knowing the sound of God's voice, simply, we are hopeless.

For the first time in twenty years I don't have a plan, and I'm learning again to wait. Waiting is difficult for someone used to anything but waiting. But the joy found in the space is indescribable.

Of course, part of the difficulty with waiting is the knowledge that something will put an end to the waiting—but something worth waiting for. Many of us would rather tuck into our own homemade plans rather than wait for the premium-quality, time-proved, God-soaked variety. So part of waiting is actually learning to trust God.

Forty years into this life, and I'm aware of just how simple my faith is. Such as this truth: All that really matters is our friendship with Jesus. *Everything* comes from that place, from the intimate friendship with our Saviour. Without that friendship, we're just flesh. Without it, we're alone.

Spending so much time on the road gets a person used to a strange way of living: You're surrounded by people who take care of all the practical concerns, and your primary goals are whiling away the dead hours and getting ready for the massive adrenaline rush from stepping onstage in front of the crowd. Being a stay-at-home parent couldn't be more different. Now life is about practicalities. There are no crowds cheering you on as you expertly cook dinner, help with four different batches of homework, and deal with a couple of tantrums at the same time. Throughout those days in the band I tried my best to be a good man to Anna and to be a great dad to my six children. At times I failed miserably, sometimes through selfishness or jet lag. Mostly I failed because I'd always leave a small part of my heart in whatever country I'd just visited.

If anyone reading this feels like they want to end up living life on the road too, then first please be sure that you—you and the ones you love—were "called" to that life. Otherwise that life will eat you up and spit you out.

Coming off the road has been bittersweet. I've spent more time in my own bed in six months than I did in the previous fifteen years. I feel better physically, haven't had jet lag for six months, and feel far more connected with my own soul. And when life moves slower you notice more around you. Recently, I discovered that my youngest daughter Mary's favourite pair of shoes are green slip-ons! I'm hearing God's voice louder than ever. Turning the volume down on the rest of life always results in God's voice sounding clearer.

But there have been difficulties. From the moment that Anna and I got married, all we've known is this crazy life of music, travel, making records, making babies, and making plans. Now we can reconnect at a deeper level and find each other again. When as a whole family you're going through a transition it's not always a bed of roses. There have been times of absolute joy and happiness at being together in a more complete way. But there have also been times of darkness as I mourn the letting go of something so good, and learn to live without the electricity of being in front of a crowd, doing what I was made to do.

I have also begun to realise how much I hurt Anna. All those little moments at the doorstep or on tour when she had to be both mum and dad to all our children, I know caused damage. Even though God was in our choices with the band, sometimes there's still a huge price to pay for the life to which we gave ourselves.

This isn't the sort of language that Anna would use, but I wonder whether at times she was dying inside. All those times I was away, all that shouldering the burdens herself, all that holiday-romance pattern where I would come and go from month to month—all the adrenaline needed to keep home life on an even keel—I think it was much harder than she ever let on. She's been incredibly faithful and supportive of me throughout the entire journey, and I've realised that in this season I can offer some of the same back to her.

Anna and I have always been close, but lately I've begun to realise just how little I really, really knew her. The more I spend time with her, the more I want to. And that's what it's like with God. I want the future to be a journey that I walk step by step with Him. Can I trust Him to do the same? Of course I know that I can, but will I act as though I do? Will I choose to trust Him? Will I trust enough to obey?

I read a great quote the other day. Ralph Waldo Emerson said, "Not in his goals but in his transitions man is great."[1]

Many of you know that things are changing. I don't mean the surface things like an impending change of government, the price of

---

1 Ralph Waldo Emerson, *The Complete Works of Ralph Waldo Emerson* (Boston and New York: Houghton, Mifflin and Co., 1904), 12:60.

the US dollar, or the state of relations between well-armed nations. No. I'm talking about a spiritual shift. It is happening right now. And whenever these changes have taken place in the past they always have produced a tidal wave that both destroys and rebuilds the current culture. I think for us in the West, this change means that while we've enjoyed years of free Western capitalism, we're now facing the very real possibility that we do not have the money to pay the rent.

I don't want to make light of the financial struggles that people are going through, but I'm excited about the changes that are coming. Why? Because I believe in a God who gave us hundreds of stories about the moments when He showed up just at the right time and in the right place: with Moses at the Red Sea, with Gideon and his "jam jar" firelights, and even with His own Son, Jesus, when He opened the eyes of a blind man.

I'm very excited because I believe God is coming. And I think God is never late. Which brings us back to waiting. How do we get through periods of uncertainty? How should we behave between the now and the not yet? How will we stick it out without resorting to our homemade plans?

When the world is changing, we simply have to fix our eyes on something that never changes. That's Jesus: unchangeable and unshakeable. I've been incredibly inspired by something I read by William Bridges. He wrote:

> [Change] is as if we launched out from a riverside dock to cross to a landing on the opposite shore— only to discover in midstream that the landing was no longer there. (And when we looked back at the

other shore, we saw that the dock we left from had
just broken loose and was heading downstream.)
[We are] stuck in transition between situations,
relationships, and identities that are themselves in
transition.[2]

This is the nature of contemporary life. Transitions begin with
an ending—whether it's the end of singleness that signals the start of
a marriage, the end of a job that signals a promotion, or the end of a
band that signals the start of a new journey. Sometimes these endings
are messy, sometimes smooth, sometimes terrifying. Often we have
to take those first steps in the predawn darkness.

I have a hunch about something. In all our busyness, in all the
"good" we do, in all the empire building of big ministry and brand-
driven churches, we must take time to press the pause button. Those
of you who are brave enough may even want to press the stop button.

Let's be with Jesus. I say that I love Him and adore Him—I built
a career around singing about it—but in all the good, sometimes I
forgot to do it. I forgot to sit on a hill and talk to Jesus. I stopped
climbing trees just to sing Him my songs, read Him my love letters.
I had learned to go to battle in the King's armour, when deep down I
was always just a shepherd boy with a sling.

Just like the story of Elisha and the borrowed axe, I'm realising
that there were times when I dropped the axe head. We grew up
as part of a movement, and we became a brand. Not that there's
anything wrong with brands, but deep down our job was to lead
an army of historymakers. I don't feel as though my contribution

2 William Bridges, *Transitions* (Cambridge, MA: Perseus Books, 1980), 4.

to the songs on some albums was as strong as it could have been. When Furious Records USA failed, we needed to get out of debt. We slashed budgets and compromised creativity, and the vision grew dark and cloudy.

We started to question our involvement, to feel resentful because the machine had to be oiled. I wondered, why am I away from my family so much of the year? If we're doing this just to make money and service the machine then how long will this really last?

Before long I realised that I was no longer waking up at night to sneak downstairs and play the piano as I used to. Instead I struggled to find a balance between the business and the calling. Nobody would have noticed, but I was desperate for air, and that lack of God-given oxygen started to impact everything: my marriage, my family, and my children. If I hadn't stopped when I did, who knows what might have been lost?

For so long I stayed busy with multiple tasks piling up on me. I grew tired towards the end, although I tried not to let it show. Deep in my soul I knew that I needed to come away from it all. I knew that I thought about Delirious? more as a brand than a band, and I didn't want life to be like that. I needed time to sit on the side of a hill and return to a place of real simplicity. I'm not there yet, not as far as I'd like to be, but I'm getting there.

After seventeen years of travelling so much, it was time to go home and rebuild the foundations for the next twenty or thirty years. What's amazing is the realisation that what's happening in the present is so beautiful that I'm worrying less about the future. Family, space, lyrics, and time with Jesus—this is enough for me right now.

This goes against the grain though. In the West, *enough* is not a word that sits well with us. It's there on our plates and in our churches. We strive for the biggest, the fastest, and the loudest, and in our struggles to manufacture so *much* we end up missing out on the basic, essential truth of spending time with God.

I'm trying to ask God how far He wants our relationship to go. I have a profoundly full relationship with my wife, so how much more of an overwhelming, intimate, all-encompassing relationship should I have with God? I should be more in love with God, and that relationship should make me more complete, even than my own marriage.

Song of Songs has been on my mind lately. It's odd and I have not worked it out yet, but there's a depth to it that transforms my view of God. What would life be like if I was fully connected to my spiritual Lover?

Being a guy is not as easy as it could be these days. I know so many men for whom being away from home is easier than being home. Work becomes the thing that we do well, and we wrap our identity in it and channel all our energies in that direction. Home can be a different matter. We're less patient, less creative, and less colour-coordinated with the family. We send the kids off to school, feeling tense, unprepared, and dressed in all the wrong clothes.

I'm not even sure that I know what it takes to be a man in 2011. The pressure to be the perfect dad, husband, head of the household, and domestic god is overwhelming. Then you add the career, the physique, and the friendships as well as the roles at church.

Maybe this level of conflict and contradiction is nothing new for some women, but it's a struggle for us men. If we go one way we can appear too strong or even chauvinistic. Take it in the other direction, and we fall into the trap of acting too weak or lacking in leadership. I know too many men who've lost their identity. I know too many with great potential but no spark of life in their eyes. Why is that?

I don't think this means that we should be happy just to shrink back into the shadows. There's a challenge ahead of us, which all comes back to that idea of friendship with Jesus. Will we dedicate ourselves to spending more time with Him? Will we decide to get to know Him better? Will we make choices that scream out just how deeply we trust God?

At times like these everything gets challenged. Will we put on the table the things we hold on to too tightly? The big career break, the success of "our" ministry, or the agenda we so carefully scripted—can we sacrifice them in favour of a closer friendship with God?

I'm rediscovering what happens when I stop and listen. Now I'm remembering how to breathe, and as I do, I'm learning that good is not the same as great. *How do we become great?* We spend time with Someone who is greater.

When all around is moving and shifting and the future is uncertain, there's no need to panic. If we find Jesus we will be so enthralled, so content that we'll forget that we're in transition anyway. If we have Him inside our lives, then the good we worried about will lose its appeal in the light of His face.

In 2 Samuel 19 we read that when David was reinstated as king he offered Mephibosheth acres of fields in return for his commitment. The boy had no interest in the land because in that moment all he cared about was being with the king. Mephibosheth said, "I am content just to have you safely back again, my lord the king!" (v. 30).

In the same way, I'm learning that God doesn't want my voice—
He just wants my heart. He just wants me.

I wrote a song recently with Nick Herbert and Tim Hughes. It's
inspired by Psalm 5, and it's called "Keep the Faith." It starts like this:

I'm laying out all the pieces of my life
On the altar I'm Your sacrifice.
Let Your fire fall, I'm waiting here.
Come and take it all, this heart of fear.

All I want is to do my Father's will
And be a voice to a world that's standing still.
I must the keep the faith, not backing down.
We must keep the faith
This is our time.
We must keep the faith.

I've heard Kevin Prosch—the first worship leader who opened
my eyes to the way things could be—say many things that I've held
on to over the years. These words, though, were some of the most
precious Kevin said: "The most powerful interchange is when God
disregards the style of the music you're crafting and starts to play on
your heartstrings instead. That's the moment when heaven touches
earth."

As songwriters we have a responsibility not to take ourselves too
seriously while at the same time taking this task of leading others in
worship very seriously. We must dedicate ourselves to writing music
that will put words in people's mouths—the sort of words that reveal

more of God, that allow His presence to settle in every atom in the air.

When we put down our desire to impress God and allow Him to invade our hearts, everything can change.

Are we hungry for that? Are we ready for it? Are we brave enough to embrace it? This is a new day, and I can't wait to see a global movement of historymakers run into the arms of God.

See you there.

ACKNOWLEDGEMENTS

To my best friend, confidante, and wife, Anna. I love you so much, you are my most favourite person in the whole world! You bring so much light and sunshine to the children and me and anyone else who has the privilege of being in your life. Our journey has brought incredible joy, but you have also sacrificed greatly to see these songs touch the world. I will always be in awe of you, and I could never have become the man I am without you.

Our six beautiful children: Elle-Anna, Noah, Indi-Anna, Levi, Ruby-Anna, and Mary-Anna. I cannot even begin to express how much you have changed my life. Your lives are each a brilliant "song" that mum and I will gladly sing forever.

To my mum and dad, Eddie and Sylvia, for such a strong and safe upbringing. The foundations you laid are immeasurable, and your selflessness is a great template for eternal living. Thank you for giving me back all those years ago.

To my in-laws, David and Heather. Thank you for letting me marry your daughter! I will never be able to repay the years you have mentored me and shown me what godly living looks like.

To my family: Paul and Pip—thank you for simply being there in the midst of our transition and being so incredibly faithful. Pete and Alison and Suzi and Giles—I have only ever felt you cheer me on; you are all completely gold.

To my band of brothers: This book is in print only because of the amazing journey we have all travelled together. Tim, you were the brains and vision behind everything; thanks for believing in those little songs years ago. Stew, your drumming moved mountains, and your selflessness became a rock. Stu G, your guitar playing moved me every time, and the songs we wrote will live on. Jon, you have a good soul; your creativity never let us "settle." Paul, you helped close the last chapter with brilliance and utmost humility. Thank you.

Huge love and respect to the wives—Becca, Sarah, Karen, and Kristen—for giving everything to this people movement.

Ben Thatcher, you are an extraordinary human being!

There are so many good people who have travelled with us for so many years whom I would like to thank.

Everyone at Arun Community Church, thanks for always being willing to road test these songs!

To Mark and Darlene Zschech, Matt and Beth Redman, Tim and Rachel Hughes, Michael and Debbie Smith, Graham and Jill Kendrick, Tony and Terri Patoto, Russ and Amanda Oliver, Billy and Caroline Kennedy, Jim Mcniesh, Brett Farrell, David Meyer, Stella Coulter, Roy Baylis, Bill Hearn, Kevin Prosch, Les Moir, Helmut and Elisabeth Kaufmann, Mathias Kaufmann, Hoda and Laura Armani, David and Christine Sutcliffe, Jon and Nicola Holmes, Ian Cattle, Trevor Michael, Sam Gibson, Lee Slater, Andy Piercy, and Andy Hutch.

To Alex Field and Cris Doornbos at David C Cook. I'm still not sure why anyone would be interested in this book, but thanks for pushing me.

To my right-hand man Clive Sherwood. You have been a rock in the midst of transition. I can never thank you enough for being the servant that you are.

Big thanks to Craig Borlase for listening to me rattle on for days and turning it all into something readable. You are a good man with a unique gift.

I want to thank the historymakers. You sing the songs as though your lives depend on them. Your energy and faith constantly move mountains.

To Jesus. Thank You for continually saving my life.

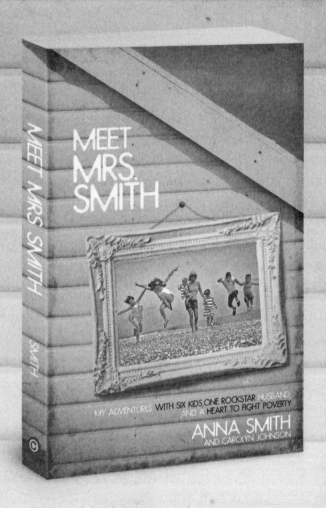

WHAT IS IT LIKE TO BE MARRIED TO A

ROCK STAR?

Anna Smith chronicles her life as wife of the lead singer of *Delirious?*, the history-making band that launched the modern-day worship movement.